jumpseat therapy 

Mindfulness Skills to Reduce Burnout and Fall Back in Love with Flying

Brian Pelletier, LPC, NCC

Table of Contents

About the Author

Brian Pelletier, LPC, NCC

Brian is a former aviation professional-turned psychotherapist. He began his aviation career as a flight attendant at ExpressJet and eventually became a ground instructor. Later, he worked as a French speaking flight attendant for Delta, based in NYC and DTW. After a workplace injury, he transitionend to the network operations center for United as a Pilot Scheduler focusing crew coordination and rerouting.

As a therapist, Brian is a NBCC Board-Certified Licensed Professional Counselor. He earned a master's degree in Clinical Mental Health Counseling from Roosevelt University in Chicago. He has worked in community, academic, high-acuity, and group practice settings. He specializes in Cognitive Behavioral approaches with a focus on mindfulness, acceptance, and radical openness. He is currently practicing at Light On Anxiety CBT Treatment Centers in Chicago.

Brian was inspired by his own relationship with burnout while working in the aviation industry. He believes crewmembers experience a unique lifestyle that can be difficult for others to conceptualize.

Why I Wrote This Book

The flight attendant lifestyle is not only unique but misunderstood by many. In fact, I find the job to have its own culture. Throughout my aviation career, I would encounter people who loved to hear all the tea about the job. However, I noticed that I was also spending a lot of time clearing up misconceptions about the occupation.

When I sought personal therapy, I noticed my therapist's assumptions about the job were often based on popular conceptions. While this book isn't for those people, I realized that flight attendants could benefit from mindfulness skills that are adapted to the field.

While learning psychotherapeutic interventions and theories in graduate school, I wondered how different my experience as a flight attendant would have been if I knew about these skills.

I hope this workbook provides my former colleagues with the skills needed to love their job in the face of corporate changes, disruptive operations, viral pandemics, distruptive passengers, and viral videos.

Selfies From Various Points In My Aviation Career
Left to Right: Earning a Private Pilots License, Working the A330 to CDG, Flight Ops

Dedicated to my cats Charlie and Henri.

And to Crystal McDowell one of my favorite ExpressJet inflight instructors whose life was tragically cut short.

1 - Preparing for Takeoff

Your phone rings at 5am, waking you from sound sleep. On the call, a voice that sounds familiar, but you've never met says, "Good morning," and tells you to be at the airport for 7am. You're going to Tampa. Begrudgingly, you roll out of bed and start packing your bag. Along with the shorts and sandals you pack for your short stay in the Sunshine State, you still pack a backup sweater and warm pants. You know your plans can change at any minute. You've had this job for ten years. This isn't your first time on reserve.

While packing you begin to think how you were assigned this trip at all. When you went to bed last night you remember seeing quite a few people ahead of you on the reserve list. What happened to all of them? You begin to wonder if scheduling selected you because you refused to extend your duty day last month. These last-minute assignments always seem to happen to you.

You meet your operating crew at the gate. You've never worked with them before but maybe you've seen them in passing. Your base has thousands of crew members so it's a treat to work with familiar faces. Despite just meeting, in about 30 minutes you will be working in a tight space with the ability to jump into action at any moment to ensure the safety of passengers and crew.

As the plane taxis to the runway for departure, your colleague looks at you from their seat and says, "I was served with divorce papers when I returned from my last trip."

If the above scenario seems all too familiar, this book is for you. Flight crew have one of the most unique occupational experiences. Success in the career requires the flexibility to handle change, the ability to take immediate action, the capacity to build instant connections with those you just met, and the capability to compartmentalize.

Flight crew also combine skills from many other professions and are prepared to use them at a moment's notice. A flight attendant can not only discuss the wine offerings on board, but they can categorize a fire, extinguish the fire, provide first aid, mediate interpersonal conflicts, deliver a baby, build a raft canopy, use an emergency transponder, offer travel advice, relocate a bomb, troubleshoot technology, train passengers to assist in an evacuation, and make a killer jack and ginger; sometimes in multiple languages. While most flight crew hope they never have to put their emergency skills to work, they get tested on them on a regular basis so that they are always ready.

The payoff for maintaining these skills is the ability to see places and cultures most people only dream about. In just one week you could be eating ramen in Tokyo, having high tea in London, and sunning in Hawaii. It's a lifestyle that is usually only accessible to the upper classes. You probably know a flight attendant or two who only buy butter in Paris. Maybe that flight attendant is you. Your life is someone's vacation.

It's not all rainbows and five-star hotels, however. This occupation takes a physical toll. Eileen McNeely and colleagues at Harvard University have published several studies on Flight Attendant health in the United States and the results paint a grim picture. Flight attendants report an increase in some cancers, cardiopulmonary concerns, mental health disorders, and sleep disorders compared to the general population (McNeely, et al. 2018). The Center for Disease Control's National Institute for Occupational Safety and Health discusses how occupational exposure to toxins (i.e.: pesticides), radiation, repetitive stress injuries, circadian rhythm disruptions, and more may play a role in these negative health outcomes (CDC, 2023). It should be noted that airline crew members have the highest exposure to ionizing radiation than other U.S. radiation workers (Maiello, 2010).

On top of all of this, there is a psychological cost. People are not machines. Life gets in the way. Our developmental, trauma, and physical histories play a role in how we respond to situations. While some duty days may feel like a walk in the park, there are other days in which just trying to keep a smile on for the passengers seems like a Sisyphean task. Whether it's an inconvenient scheduling call, a micromanaging purser, an authoritarian captain, a demanding passenger, or a distrustful partner at home; some days feel like you're fighting a one-person battle against the universe.

Despite always being around people, flight crew will tell you that the job can be very isolating. At larger airlines, crew members often meet each other for the first time when boarding the aircraft. Being surrounded by hundreds of people yet not knowing a single person can provoke feelings of isolation. The isolation continues as a crew member arrives at their layover hotel. The distance from home can feel infinite when a crew member has a partner, children, pets, or other family responsibilities back home. Junior crew members are often required to work on holidays and may not get an option to select days off to attend family events. Crew members who are parents may experience conflicts in the home regarding parental responsibilities and authority because "you're never around". A romantic partner who does not understand the job can become an added stressor if they have an insecure attachment style.

Occupational stress has been increasing for flight attendants. Unruly passenger incidents in the United States reached a record high in 2021 and continue to be at unacceptably high levels ever since. In 2022, the FAA levied over $8 million in fines to passengers for unruly behavior (Federal Aviation Administration, 2023). It seems like every few days there is a new viral video of an airline passenger having a meltdown. With the addition of operational breakdowns, record passenger enplanements, expired labor contracts, and increasing weather delays due to climate change, crew are reaching burnout faster than ever (Climate Central, 2022).

Besides violent passengers, sexual harassment is also a concern for flight attendants. The Association of Flight Attendants-

CWA (2024), a labor union representing flight attendants across many airlines, released survey results that state 68% of flight attendants have experienced sexual harassment at work while only 7% have reported the harassment to their employers. The occupation has historically been sexualized since its inception; yet despite the commodification of air travel, the harassment continues.

Access to mental health providers is another issue affecting flight crew. Although most airline employees receive comprehensive health insurance that cover mental wellness, there are systemic factors that create barriers to accessing. For all crew members, an irregular schedule can make it difficult to set up regular weekly appointments with a therapist. Being on reserve doesn't help this situation either. Additionally, state licensure laws may prevent some mental health professionals from providing care while crew members are on layover outside of their home state. Currently, several professional advocacy groups are lobbying to create licensure recognition across state lines.

Despite all this doom and gloom, there are techniques and skills we can implement to build resilience and increase satisfaction. For some, it can feel impossible to navigate out of a state of burnout or dissatisfaction. If we've started your journey in this industry many moons ago, we may not even know how to find our way back to that excited person taking our first flight. The first step in finding our way back is to figure out where we started and where are are now. Welcome to Jumpseat Therapy!

Exercise 1-A
Scheduled vs Actual Departure

For this exercise we will compare your career expectations to reality. Take a moment and return to the moment you submitted your application for your first airline crew job. What were the circumstances that brought you to that decision? For some, this is a career that was dreamed about since childhood. For others, it may have been a need for change. While contemplating this career, you may have fantasized about how your life would be as a crew member. It's okay if your imagination was naïve. Overestimating future happiness is something we do to help motivate ourselves to take action.

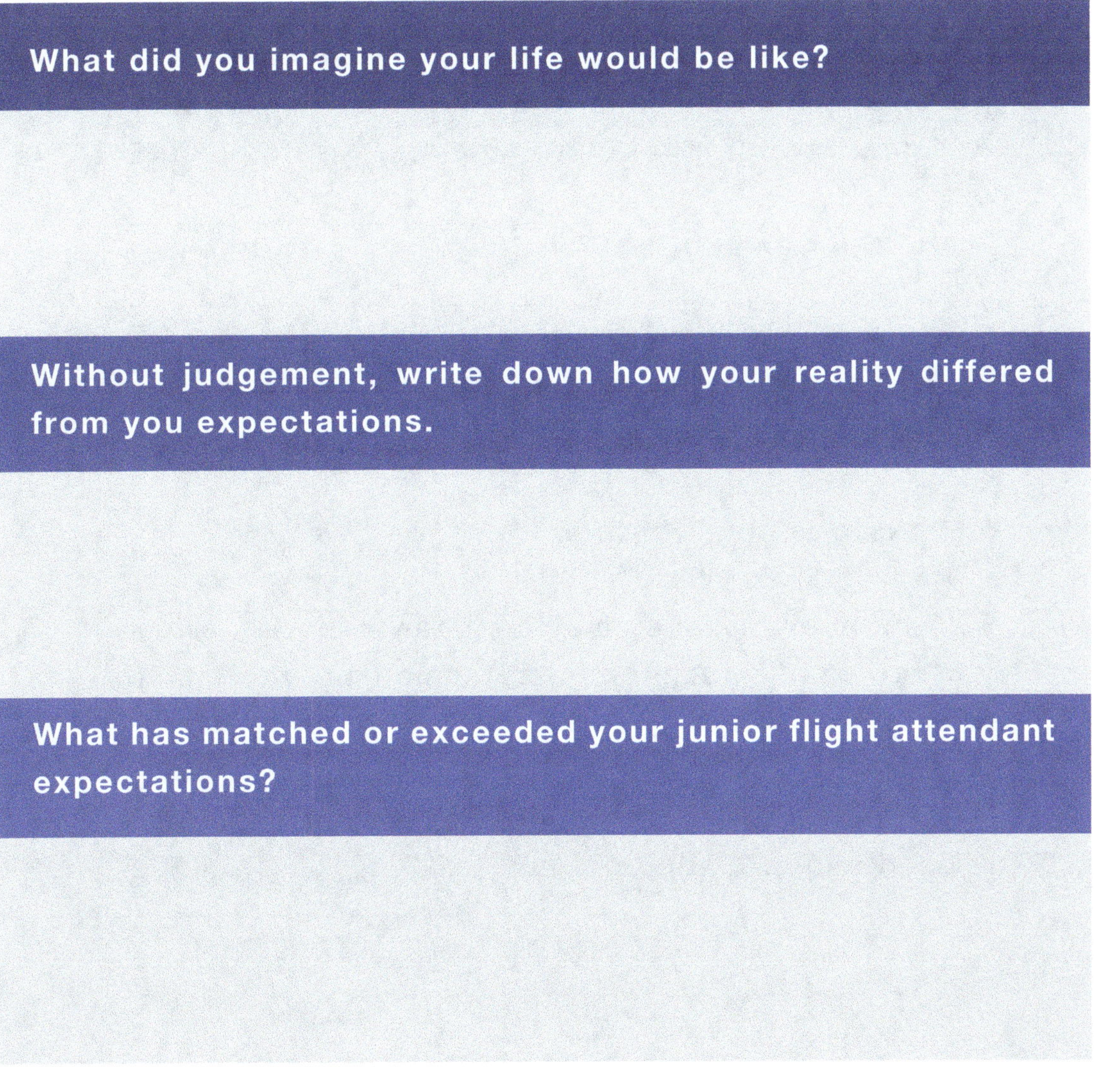

Exercise 1-B
Grounding Through Breathing

In this exercise, we will manipulate our breathing patterns to calm our nervous system. Our breathing patterns can affect our engagement with the environment. When we use shallow breaths or high into our chest, our mind perceives possible threat. However, when we breathe deep into our belly, we begin to relax and connect with the present moment.

1. Score whatever tension you are feeling from 0-10.

2. Breathe in through your nose to a count of five. Be sure to breathe deep down into your diaphragm to signal to your mind that you are in a safe place.

3. Hold for a count of four.

4. Breathe out through your mouth to a count of seven. Be sure to breathe out all the air as if you are deflating an air mattress.

5. Hold for a count of four.

6. Continue this exercise for a few rounds. When you are ready, recheck your tension by scoring it from zero to ten.

7. If the score is still too high, repeat until you feel relaxed and grounded.

Exercise 1-C
Countdown Sensory Grounding

Engaging our senses is another great way to ground to the present moment and calm our nervous system. In this exercise, we will engage all five senses.

5 Look around you. Name five things you can see. Don't just see them. Say the objects either outloud or to yourself.

4 Take a moment and listen to your environment. Name four things you can hear. Notice each one individually.

3 Tune into your sense of touch. Can you name three things you can physically feel? Use your hands or simply feel the way your clothes are on your body.

2 Take a nice deep breath in through your nose. What do you smell? Name two things you can smell. Don't do this in the lavatory.

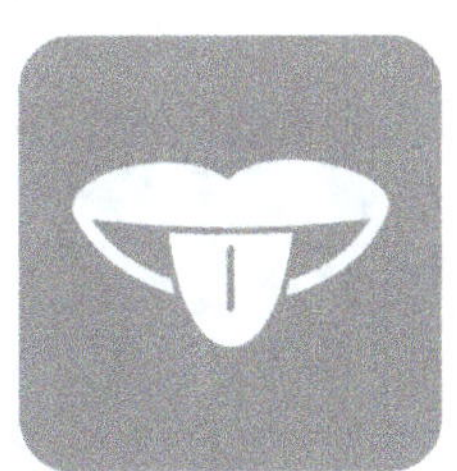

1 Tune inward towards your mouth. What can you taste? If you can't taste anything, eat something. Describe the flavor.

Exercise 1-D
Bag of Pretzels

This exercise combines using an object to ground to the present as well as mindful eating. If you don't have a bag of pretzels, any small food item you can hold in your hand will do.

1. Take a bag or pretzels or other packaged passenger snack.

2. Observe the package with your senses. Look at the colors and the print. What do you see?

3. Hear the crinkle of the packaging. Shake the bag and hear the rustle of the contents.

4. Feel the air trapped in the bag, the texture of the packaging, and the temperature.

5. Go ahead and open the bag.

6. Look at the contents. Take a deep breath and take in the aroma.

7. Take a pretzel out and observe it. Notice the shape, the twist, and the texture.

8. Place the pretzel in your mouth. What do you feel? What do you taste? Move it around with your tongue.

9. Hear the crunching sound as you eat it. Repeat.

Exercise 1-E
That Was Then... This Is Now

Compare and contrast where you were at the start of your aviation career to where you are now.

	Age	
	Airline	
	Base	
	Where Did You Live	
	Relationship Status	
	Favorite Aircraft	
	Favorite Layover	
	Dream Vacation	
	Salary	
	Car	
	Best Friend	
	Favorite Cuisine	

Exercise 1-F
Your Favorite Trip

Take a moment to reflect back on your career. Out of all the trips you have worked, one must stand out as your favorite trip. What was it about that trip that made it so awesome? Was it the crew, passengers, layover, or something else? Write your story below:

Exercise 1-G
The Perfect Trip

Now that you've recalled your favorite trip, let's get aspirational. Write down the details of what would make the perfect trip to work. Is there anything you can do to make this actually happen?

Exercise 1-H
A Letter from the Future

Scientists have recently discovered how to send letters to the past. Write a letter or a motivational message to yourself on your first duty day as a flight attendant. What encouragement would that junior flight attendant need to hear in that moment?

Exercise 1-H
A Letter from the Future

2 - Recognizing Burnout

You have just finished boarding a transcontinental flight. It's Spring Break so every seat is taken. The overhead bins were full before Zone 2. Before the door closes, you notice someone with a large purse on their lap. You advise them that the bag needs to go under the seat in front of them. The passenger says, "uh huh," and starts to put the bag under seat.

During your final walkthrough, you notice the passenger is now wearing a large hoodie. At first glance, it seems like the purse you asked to be stowed is now hidden under the hoodie. In fact, you see the designer strap sticking out of the bottom. What do you do?

DC_studio/EnvatoElements

Even though there may be a standard answer in your manual, the way you answer this question can reveal a lot about the current state of your career and your state of burnout. If you had just come back from vacation or a new hire, you may not even think twice about reminding the passenger to properly stow their bag. Your stress level is lower, so a simple request doesn't feel like a confrontation. However, you if have been flying high time all season, you may just look the other way and continue to your jumpseat. Every flight there always seems to be a passenger that wants to argue. Besides, no one listens to you anyway and you are just too tired to ask twice.

In this chapter, we will discuss burnout and compassion fatigue. You may be familiar with the concept of burnout. But, what is compassion fatigue?

Compassion fatigue is one of the many causes of burnout among flight attendants. The concept is often talked about among those in the helping professions such as healthcare workers, first responders, and teachers. However, being a flight attendant requires a lot of empathy, too. Passengers board your aircraft for a variety of reasons from business trips to vacations to funerals. It takes powerful skills to be able to cater to this diversity of needs. It can be easy to fall into the trap of continually giving to others without regard to us. It feels like the right thing to do even if it is exhausting.

Let's discuss the various phases of compassion fatigue and relate them to phases of the flight attendant career. (Newell & Mac-Neil, 2010).

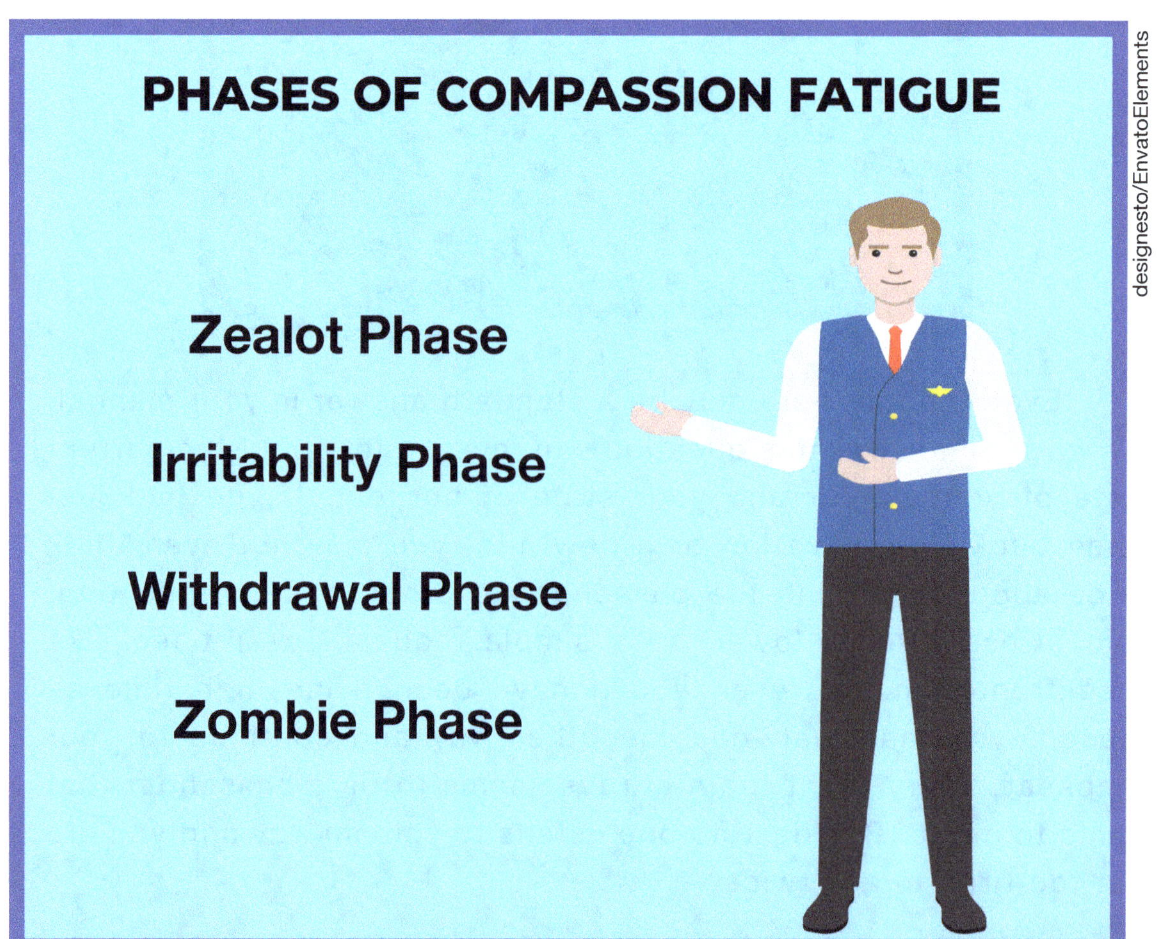

Zealot Phase

In the zealot phase of compassion fatigue, flight attendants may find themselves experiencing an intense and driven commitment to their work. They might feel an overwhelming sense of responsibility to meet every passenger's needs, going above and beyond their duties. This heightened dedication can be fueled by a genuine desire to provide exceptional service.

Characteristics of the Zealot Phase

Excessive Engagement:
Flight attendants in the zealot phase may become excessively engaged in their work, often neglecting personal boundaries. They might volunteer for extra trips, take on additional responsibilities, or prioritize passengers' needs over their own well-being.

Heightened Emotional Investment:
There is a deep emotional investment in the job, where flight attendants may absorb the emotional experiences of passengers. While empathy is a valuable trait, during the zealot phase, this emotional absorption can become overwhelming.

Neglecting Self-Care:
Flight attendants in the zealot phase may neglect self-care practices. They might put their own needs on the back burner, thinking that taking care of passengers is more important. This neglect can contribute to emotional and physical exhaustion.

An Example:
Imagine the zealot phase as a flight attendant who sees a passenger in distress during turbulence. The instinct to help and ensure the passenger's comfort is strong. In the zealot phase, this instinct becomes so intense that the flight attendant, despite the dangerous conditions in the cabin, continues to offer assistance without taking a break or considering their own well-being.

Impact on Performance:
While the zealot phase is driven by a genuine commitment to service, it can lead to burnout, workplace injuries, and a decline in overall performance. Flight attendants may find it challenging to maintain the same level of enthusiasm and effectiveness, as the exhaustion accumulates.

Describe Your Experience in the Zealot Phase

Irritability Phase

In the irritability phase of compassion fatigue, flight attendants may experience heightened irritability, impatience, and frustration. The cumulative stress and emotional toll of consistently meeting the demands of passengers can manifest in changes in mood and temperament.

Characteristics of the Irritability Phase:

Shortened Fuse:
Flight attendants in the irritability phase may find that their patience wears thin more quickly than usual. What might have been a minor inconvenience in the past could now trigger a stronger emotional response.

Increased Frustration:
There is a heightened sense of frustration, particularly when faced with challenging passengers, unforeseen issues, or disruptions to the usual routine. Flight attendants may feel overwhelmed by the constant need to manage various stressors.

Difficulty Coping:
Coping mechanisms that flight attendants typically rely on may become less effective during the irritability phase. Stressors that were once manageable may now seem more challenging to handle. There may be an urge to immediately "check-out" with substances at the end of your duty.

An Example:
Imagine the irritability phase as a flight attendant dealing with a series of minor disruptions during a flight. Each additional stressor contributes to a growing sense of frustration. Perhaps you feel tension when a passenger asks you for an extra napkin immediately after you started pushing your cart to the next position.

Impact on Performance:
The irritability phase can affect overall job performance. Flight attendants may find it more challenging to maintain the same level of calm and courtesy, potentially leading to strained interactions with passengers and colleagues.

Describe Your Experience in the Irritability Phase

Withdrawal Phase

In the withdrawal phase of compassion fatigue, flight attendants may experience a sense of emotional numbness or detachment. The continuous exposure to the emotional needs of passengers and the challenges of the job can lead to a protective emotional withdrawal.

Characteristics of the Withdrawal Phase:

Emotional Detachment:
Flight attendants in the withdrawal phase may notice a gradual emotional detachment from their work. They might find it challenging to connect with the emotions of passengers or feel a reduced sense of empathy.

Decreased Job Satisfaction:
There is a decline in overall job satisfaction as flight attendants may start to feel less motivated or engaged in their work. The emotional toll may lead to a sense of apathy or indifference.

Isolation:
Flight attendants may withdraw socially, both at work and in personal life. They might limit interactions with colleagues and friends, seeking solitude as a way to cope with emotional fatigue. If we have gone from the occasional slam-click to co-cooning every trip, you may be experiencing this phase.

An Example:
During a tarmac delay, a passenger rings their call bell. When you respond, the passenger expresses concern about their connection. They explain that they are on their way to a family funeral. You look at the passenger and say, "There's nothing we can do about it now." Returning to the galley, you suspect the passenger was just making up a sob story to manipulate you.

Impact on Performance:
The withdrawal phase can impact overall job performance, with flight attendants potentially providing service in a more routine or detached manner. The emotional disengagement may affect the quality of interactions with passengers and colleagues.

Describe Your Experience in the Withdrawal Phase

Zombie Phase

In the zombie phase of compassion fatigue, flight attendants may experience a profound sense of emotional and physical exhaustion. This phase is characterized by a feeling of going through the motions without genuine emotional engagement. Flight attendants may feel like "zombies" in their roles, displaying automatic responses and a lack of enthusiasm.

Characteristics of the Zombie Phase:

Emotional Exhaustion:
Flight attendants in the zombie phase may feel emotionally drained, experiencing a sense of numbness or indifference towards their work. The once vibrant and caring approach to passengers may be replaced by a robotic routine.

Physical Fatigue:
There is a notable increase in physical fatigue, with flight attendants feeling exhausted both mentally and physically. The demands of the job, combined with the emotional toll, contribute to a sense of weariness.

Automatic Responses:
Flight attendants may find themselves going through their tasks automatically, without the same level of thoughtfulness or engagement. Interactions with passengers and colleagues may become routine, lacking the usual warmth and connection.

An Example:
Imagine the zombie phase as a flight attendant moving through the cabin on autopilot. Perhaps your pre-flight safety checks or cabin walkthroughs are just performative without noticing safety concerns. The emotional batteries, like those of a zombie, are drained, leading to a sense of automatic functioning.

Impact on Performance:
The zombie phase significantly impacts job performance, with flight attendants potentially providing service in a more mechanical and detached manner. The risk of burnout is high, and safety can be compromised.

Describe Your Experience in the Zombie Phase

Quick Tips To Combat Compassion Fatigue

- Create boundaries to increase work/life balance.
- Utilize support options such as peer support or employee assistance programs.
- Avoid airline related social media on your days off.
- Consider a special assignment position to decrease your time in the air.
- Change your type of flying (i.e.: work economy instead of business, bid short-haul instead of long-haul).
- Utilize your on-board team and avoid being a lone wolf.
- Engage in daily mindfulness practice.
- If your flight has a scheduled crew break, use it.
- Keep track of strong reactions on duty and look for common triggers and stressors.
- Stay hydrated.
- When on vacation consider accessing your ZED/jumpseat benefits on another airline to create a separation between leisure and work.
- Combat stress with exercise after every duty day.
- Take advantage of the preventative care benefits included in your employee health plan.
- Don't add to your duties. Consistency is key.
- Safety above all. Stop service if conditions are too dangerous.

- ____.

- ____.

- ____.

- ____.

Exercise 2-A
Compassion Fatigue

Read the vignettes below and decide which phase of compassion fatigue the flight attendant is experiencing. (Zealot, Irritability, Withdrawal, Zombie).

After finishing beverage service for a row, a passenger who was just served asks, "Can I also have a glass of water?" The flight attendant rolls their eyes and sigh while pour a glass of water. They avoid eye contact while passing the cup and immediately release the cart break to move on.

PHASE: ___________________________

A flight attendant boards an aircraft for their third transoceanic leg this week. It's summer. After stowing their luggage they open the bin of their assigned emergency equipment. "It looks like it's all there. Good enough for me," they say.

PHASE: ___________________________

The captain briefs the crew that this flight will be bumpy and she doubts if it will be safe to serve the passengers. Twenty minutes after take off, the flight attendant decides to serve first class despite the turbulence. They want impress the passengers with their commitment to service.

PHASE: ___________________________

During boarding, a flight attendant decides to hide in the galley and break ice. A passenger comes to the galley with an empty coffee cup. The flight attendant points to the trash bin without saying a word.

PHASE: ___________________________

Answer Key: 1:Irritability, 2:Zombie, 3:Zealot, 4:Withdrawal

Signs of Burnout

Headaches	Rigid Thinking
Muscle tension	Insomnia
Increased Illness	Hopelessness
Exhaustion	Dread About Work
Loss of appetite	Feeling Trapped
Increased Substance Use	Anhedonia
Depression	Loss of Motivation
Anxiety	Depersonalization
Cynicism	Detachment
Anger	Helplessness
Decreased Concentration	Isolation
Increased Risk Taking	Resentment

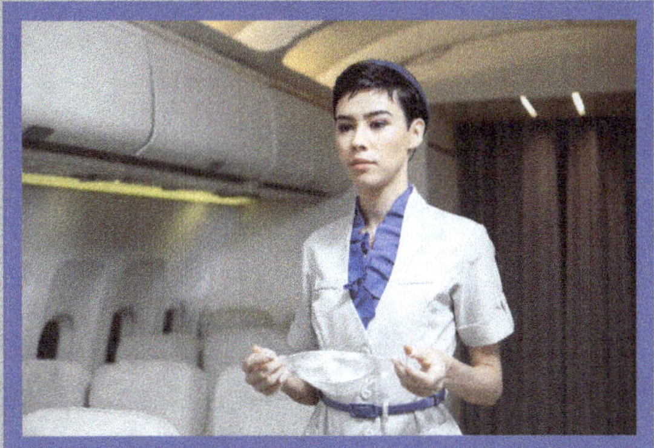

winnievinzence/EnvatoElements

Exercise 2-B
Recognizing Your Burnout Signs

Burnout can manifest itself physically, emotionally, and behaviorally. Being aware of our stress reactions can allow us to take protective action before we go too far. Take a moment to recall your most stressful duty day in recent memory.

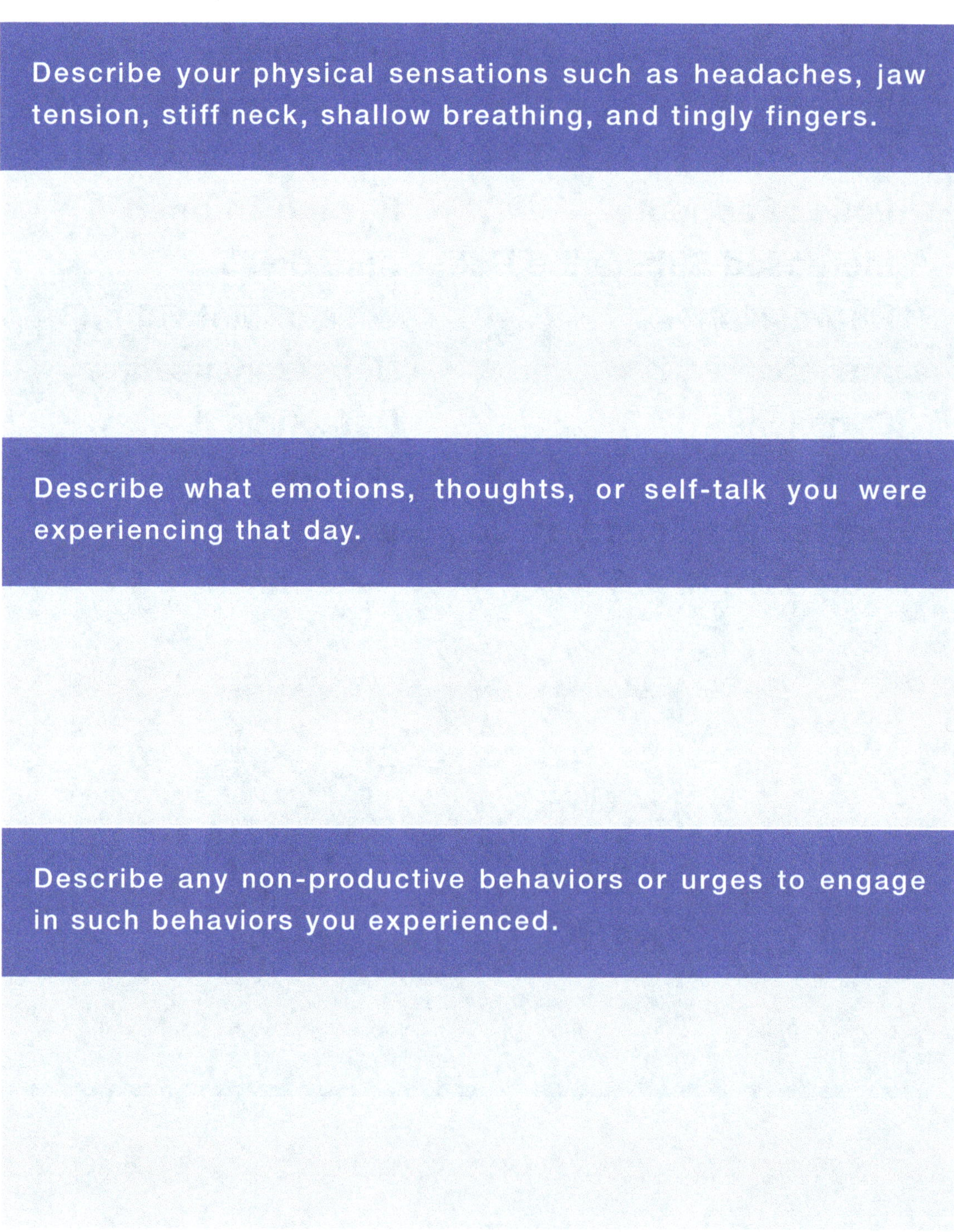

Exercise 2-C
Burnout Inventory

Rate the following statements to determine your chances of burnout using a 1 to 5 scale:
(1 - never, 2 - rarely, 3 - sometimes, 4 - very often, 5 - always).

1. I feel physically exhausted before I start a trip. ______

2. Basic requests from passengers irritate me.
(ie: Where is my seat?) ______

3. It's hard for me to believe anything a passenger says. ______

4. I experience a feeling of dread before starting a trip. ______

5. I get easily irritated with coworkers. ______

6. I find ways to "punish" passengers that irritate me. ______

7. I wonder if I'm in the wrong job/profession. ______

8. I resist change at work. ______

9. I don't feel appreciated by my company. ______

10. I have less sympathy for others than I used to. ______

TOTAL ______

Total available points 50.
A low score may indicate less chance of burnout.
A high score may indicate high chance of burnout.

Exercise 2-D
Get Some A.I.R.

Some days, we wake up and notice our fuse is a little short. Things that don't normally bother us now seem challenging. In those times, it's time to get some air. Sure, getting fresh air on an airplane is impossible. So, for these situations we'll use the acronym A.I.R.

A - Acknowledge your distress.

Label your feeling. Put a name to it.

I - Introspection.

Ask yourself what about this situation is bothering you.
How do I want to be perceived in this situation?
Is it possible I don't have all the information I need to react?
Am I getting involved in tit-for-tat pettiness?

R - Respond

Now that you have taken a moment to reflect, mindfully respond.

3 - Using Your Compass

Imagine you are just coming to the end of your days off. Now it's time to commute back to base for a couple back-to-back trips. As you pack your bag, you contemplate if you are going to explore on your layovers or have a slam-click marathon. You take many factors into consideration. Have you been to this layover in the past? What's your budget like? Who is on your crew? Does the hotel have a pool? You look at the weather report. Another cold and rainy day in Shannon. You pack some comfortable clothes and prepare to binge watch your favorite show and order room service.

FabrikaPhoto/EnvatoElements

Before you make your way to the airport to commute to base, you look at the flight loads one last time. It seems the flights have filled up. Last night, your commute looked easy but now there is a chance you may not make your first flight. You begin to explore your options: a two-leg commute, taking a jumpseat, listing on another airline, or buying a confirmed ticket. You weigh your options against your comfort, finances, and experience. Perhaps you recently had to use your company's commuter clause last month and don't want to use it again so soon. Or your contract has a great commuter policy, but you buddy bid this trip and don't want to let your friend down.

Hundreds of times a day we are faced with choices. Some are rather benign like choosing what flavor creamer to put in our coffee. Other decisions may have a larger impact such as bidding for a base transfer. No matter the size of the dilemma, in the fast-paced world of aviation, clarity of purpose is not just a luxury; it's a necessity. Just as a well-defined flight plan is crucial for a smooth journey, understanding and aligning decisions to our core values is essential for a fulfilling and purpose-driven life and career. In other words, we need to consider our values so that we make decisions that move us closer to our goals.

Why is this important? Much like a seasoned pilot anticipates turbulence, understanding our values helps us navigate life's challenges with resilience. When we are grounded in our values, we can weather the storms in personal and professional arenas. Additionally, our values serve as fuel that propels us forward to our goals, just like jet fuel gets the plane to its destination. Connecting with our values provides the sustainable energy needed for the long hours and demanding situations crew encounter each duty day.

What do you think of when you hear the word values? Some people use values as a political buzzword often synonymous with morality. For others, values are qualities you aspire to live by. This is probably the definition your airline uses when discussing company values. For the purposes of acceptance and mindfulness, values are how you want to behave, treat yourself, and treat others right now (Harris, 2019). Notice that we are asking ourselves, 'how we want to live now' instead of 'what we want to do.' Values are right now; goals are in the future.

Values and Bidding

To illustrate how values play a role in our decisions, think of your values like bidding for your monthly trips. When you first started flying, you may have been on reserve or assigned a line by the company. Essentially, the airline is giving you assignments that work best for the operation. Likewise, your first set of values was probably handed to you. We are told what is important by our family, culture, school, and religion. We also see people whom we respect and emulate the qualities we admire in them. As seniority grows, you can have more determination over your schedule. In life, as we get older and differentiate from our families, we are able to replace values given to us with ones that we find more beneficial.

How we apply our values can be compared how we decide to bid out schedule each month. If you use a Preferential Bidding

System (PBS) you may score various factors to fit your needs. Each situation may call for prioritization of our values in a different order. For example, while financial stability may be important to you, you know there's an important family event coming up next month so you can't bid high time to make sure you're available for the event. In this case, you are valuing family, togetherness, fidelity, or other similar values over financial stability. The following month you may have taxes due and decide to fly high time rather than bid around your niece's sweet sixteen party. In either case, we are calling on our values to ensure our decisions align with our goals.

designesto/EnvatoElements

Exercise 3-A
Who Do You Admire?

This exercise is designed to help you determine your values by recognizing exemplary qualities in those you admire.

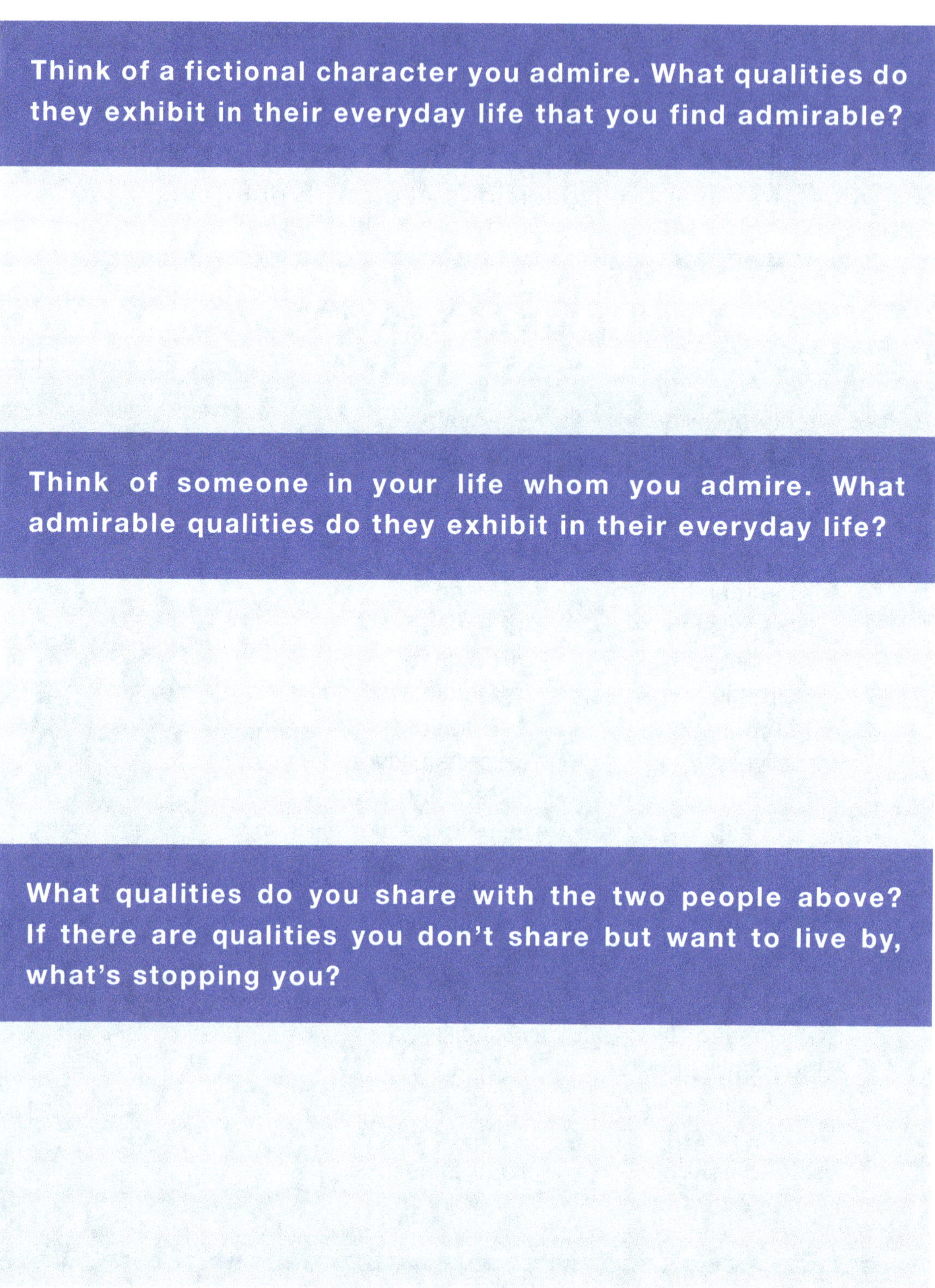

Exercise 3-B
Retirement Party

drazenphoto/EnvatoElements

After countless years and millions of miles in the sky, you've decided to hang up your wings. Your closest friends from work decide to throw you a retirement party. Each one gets up to make a speech about your career and your personality. What would they say about you? Find the core values in their statements and write them down.

Exercise 3-C
Evacuate! Evacuate! Evacuate!

When identifying your values, sometimes we can look at who and what is important to us. The following exercise is designed to do just that.

You are working a flight in which the only passengers are your loved ones (family, friends, pets, etc.). In the cargo hold are all your possessions. Upon landing, an engine catches fire and the captain calls for an evacuation. All the passenger seatbelts malfunction. You have time to rescue three people. Who will you rescue?

Who did you rescue and why?

Good news! Firefighters rescued everyone. They say they can rescue three items from cargo. What items will you choose and why?

Real_life_Studio/EnvatoElements

Exercise 3-D
Values Fusion

While we strive to live by our values, we need to be mindful not to become fused with our values. If we become stuck on our values, we may miss out on opportunities to learn and grow. For example, let's say you identified independence and self-reliance as values. If you fuse with these values to the point of not accepting help from others, it could be detrimental in certain situations. Use this exercise to identify times when you fused with a value.

Reflect on a time you were fused with a value. How did it affect you? What did you learn?

Exercise 3-E
Values Check-In

Now that you've identified your values. Let's check-in to see if your actions and values are aligned. Review each life domain below and score the consistentcy of your actions to values.

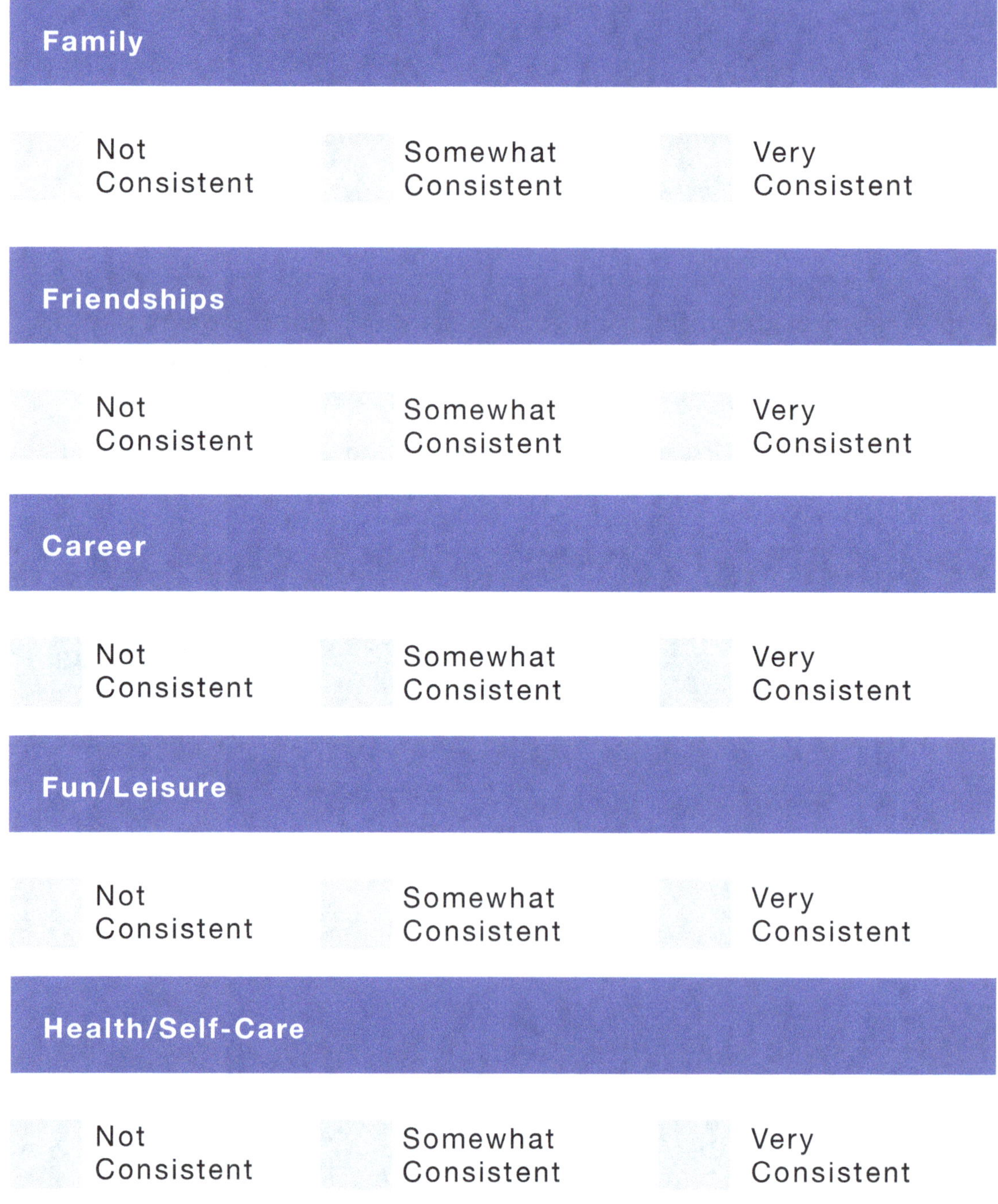

Family

Not Consistent   Somewhat Consistent   Very Consistent

Friendships

Not Consistent   Somewhat Consistent   Very Consistent

Career

Not Consistent   Somewhat Consistent   Very Consistent

Fun/Leisure

Not Consistent   Somewhat Consistent   Very Consistent

Health/Self-Care

Not Consistent   Somewhat Consistent   Very Consistent

Exercise 3-F
Values To Action

Choose three values from the list of value words in Chapter 3. Then decide the action you can take this week to live according to each value.

Value 1	Value 2	Value 3

What Can You Do This Week To Live By Value 1?

What Can You Do This Week To Live By Value 2?

What Can You Do This Week To Live By Value 3?

Exercise 3-G
Waiting for the Perfect Plane

Imagine you are about to take part in a dream vacation. You've always wanted to go to this destination but never had the opportunity or the means until you became a flight attendant.

After months of planning, you arrive at the airport for your flight. You see two aircraft going to the same destination, the hub in which you need to connect. The first aircraft is a narrowbody plane with standard two-class seating. The second aircraft is a new widebody with lie-flat suites in the premium cabin.

You want the upgrade and decide to wait for the fancy plane. While you are waiting, you see the narrowbody board and depart. The widebody plane gets delayed and another narrowbody boards and departs. Still, you insist on a perfect vacation and wait for the widebody jet. By the time it boards, three narrowbody jets have departed and there is a chance you may miss your connection.

Take a moment to reflect what actions in your life are you delaying waiting for the perfect conditions. What's stopping you from getting on your way in a narrowbody jet?

4 - The Control Tower

After working three flights, you are finally landing in New Orleans and ready for your layover. There's something about the Cajun cuisine, live music, and people watching that make the Crescent City one of your favorite layovers. When you saw this trip with a thirty-hour stay, you knew you had to bid for it. As the plane turns onto the taxiway, you take your personal phone off airplane mode. Immediately, it starts vibrating with notifications.

ChrisFloresFoto/EnvatoElements

Before you can even check your notifications, your phone starts ringing. It's crew scheduling. You know the rules. You're not going to answer from the jumpseat. Still, you have an ominous feeling that changes are coming. When the boarding door opens, the gate agent asks you to call scheduling and to not leave the airport. You say goodbye to the remaining passengers and proceed to find out what all the notifications are about. The crew scheduled to take your plane is delayed. The airline wants you to operate the outbound flight. In an instant, your dreams of gumbo, red beans and rice, and fried green tomatoes vanish.

This scenario plays out countless times a day in the airline industry. It's one of the more frustrating parts of the job. It's even more challenging if, in the last chapter, you identified "autonomy" or "predictability" as core values. Change is the only constant in this career. In order for us to embrace change, we must give up control.

The entire air travel experience is about giving up control. Whether you are a crew member or a passenger, there are countless variables that can affect your trip. Even if you plan every detail of your journey, you are at the mercy of weather, air traffic, mechanical problems, staffing shortages, and more. While you may have picked up a three-day trip to London, a volcanic eruption in Iceland may extend your stay for a week.

Even though you know this is part of the lifestyle, regular schedule disruptions can frustrate even the most seasoned of flight attendants. This can lead to burnout and overall life dissatisfaction. To combat this, we need to train our minds to be more flexible to change. We can do this through mindfulness. Let's start by accepting what we can and cannot control.

wirestock/EnvatoElements

The Seatbelt Sign

As humans we have tremendous influence on our environment. This influence can give us a false sense that we have full control over external factors. To the contrary, there are countless external variables also influencing these factors. Therefore, it's best to give up the idea that we have control and instead think about how we can influence external factors.

Think of it this way. Halfway through your flight, you encounter some moderate turbulence. The captain turns on the seatbelt sign and the appropriate announcements are made. You secure the galley and return to your jumpseat. Moments pass and you see a passenger in the aisle making their way to the lavatory. You make a follow-up announcement reminding passengers that the fasten seatbelt sign is still illuminated. Can you actually stop the passenger from making their way to the lavatory? Not really. You only have influence on others but not control.

How much control do we have over ourselves? To test our level of personal control, let's break down the human experience into three domains: thoughts, emotions, and behavior. The following exercises are designed to build understanding of how much control we really have.

Exercise 4-A
Don't Think Puppies!

Set a timer for two minute. You may start it now. During this time, do not think about puppies. Absolutely, do not think about puppies no matter how cute you think they are. Thinking about puppies is forbidden. Spend the rest of your time not thinking about puppies. How did you do?

Did you notice that the more you fought, the harder it became to resist thinking about puppies? That's normal. Now, try the exercise again and only think about puppies for the first minute and kittens for the second minute. How did you do? You may have noticed it's much easier to accept than to resist. Why is that? Move on to the next exercise to find out.

Exercise 4-B
Baggage Carousel

maxxyustas/EnvatoElements

Imagine your brain is like the baggage infrastructure at the busiest hub in your airline's network. Each piece of luggage is like a piece of information, stimulus, or thought. Behind-the-scenes there are thousands of bags coming in, being processed, and going out. Most of these bags never leave the secured area as they are connecting to other flights.

Now we arrive at baggage claim where the bags are available to claim. Do we need to inspect every bag that moves along the belt? Probably not. We can do that with our mind, too. Our brain is constantly generating new thoughts and not all of them require interaction. Some thoughts like negative self-talk may have been placed there by others; much like a suitcase that looks like ours but is tagged with someone else's name.

Take a moment to get in a comfortable position, take a few deep breaths, and close your eyes. Now clear your mind and imagine an empty conveyor belt. As new thoughts pop into your brain, don't fight them. Instead, just let them pass like bags on the carousel. You can also use this exercise to slow your mind down when you find your thoughts racing.

Exercise 4-C
Emotional Memory

Now, let's focus on emotions. Just like our thoughts, emotions can arise pretty quickly. As professionals who interact with the public, most flight attendants have stories in which they had to "bite their tongue" when dealing with an emotionally charged situation on board. Do you have an example in your mind?

Take a moment and recall that story, either to yourself or out loud to a trusted person. Do you notice how the emotions you felt in the story are now showing up in the present?

Galyna_Andrushko/EnvatoElements

Exercise 4-D
Turbulent Skies

Imagine your emotions as the skies you navigate while on duty. Just like the ever-changing weather conditions during a flight, emotions can sometimes be turbulent and unpredictable. You can't control the weather, just as you can't control the turbulence that might arise in your emotional journey. Turbulence is a natural part of the flight, and emotions are a natural part of the human experience.

While you can't control the turbulence itself, you have control over how you respond to it. In moments of emotional turbulence, rather than trying to control or suppress the emotions, imagine acknowledging them as you would acknowledge turbulence during a flight. Feel the emotions, let them pass through, and trust your values to guide you safely. Like a skilled pilot navigating through the clouds, your awareness and acceptance become your instruments for a smoother emotional journey.

Exercise 4-E
Pavlov's Stew

Weedezign_photo/EnvatoElements

If you've studied psychology, you may have learned about Pavlov's Dog. Using a bell and food, Pavlov was able to condition his dog to engage in an automatic behavior, in this case salivate, by associating the sound of the bell to being fed.

Flight Attendant training is built around this type of conditioning. When you hear your airline's brace command, you know exactly what to do without stopping to think. The next time you're on a plane, watch where your eyes go when you hear a call bell. Can you recall other automatic behaviors that you have been conditioned to perform? Fill out the behavior chain below.

Stimulus

Heard a notification chime.

Thought/Emotion

I must have received a text.

Action

Checked my phone.

Exercise 4-F
Urge Surfing

Unlike thoughts and emotions which come on quickly, we are given a more control of our behaviors. Even in a Pavlovian situation like a call bell chime, you still have time to decide what to do next.

Austrian Psychiatrist Viktor Frankl, who personally experienced and witnessed the horrors of the concentration camps of World War II, stated, "Between stimulus and response there is a space. In that space is our power to choose our response. In our response lies our growth and our freedom."

Through Urge Surfing, we can increase the space between stimulus and response. It is a technique we can use when the urge to act is strong, but we know there will be detrimental consequences for the behavior. Examples include engaging with an unruly passenger, arguing on social media, substance use, checking the trade board on your day off, and addictive behaviors. Let's give it a try.

Name the urge and rate the intensity 0-10.

Now, set a timer for 5 minutes. During this time, you can either meditate or engage in another activity that isn't related to the urge you are trying to extinguish (i.e.: watching television, reading a book, going for a walk, listening to music). For powerful urges, set the timer to 30 minutes.

Re-rate your urge intensity 0-10.

If the intensity went down, congratulations. If not, try again with a longer time set or engage in another mindfulness activity.

Exercise 4-G
On Your Radar

Use the graphic below to visualize areas in your life you can control, areas in which you can influence, and areas where you can give up the struggle for control.

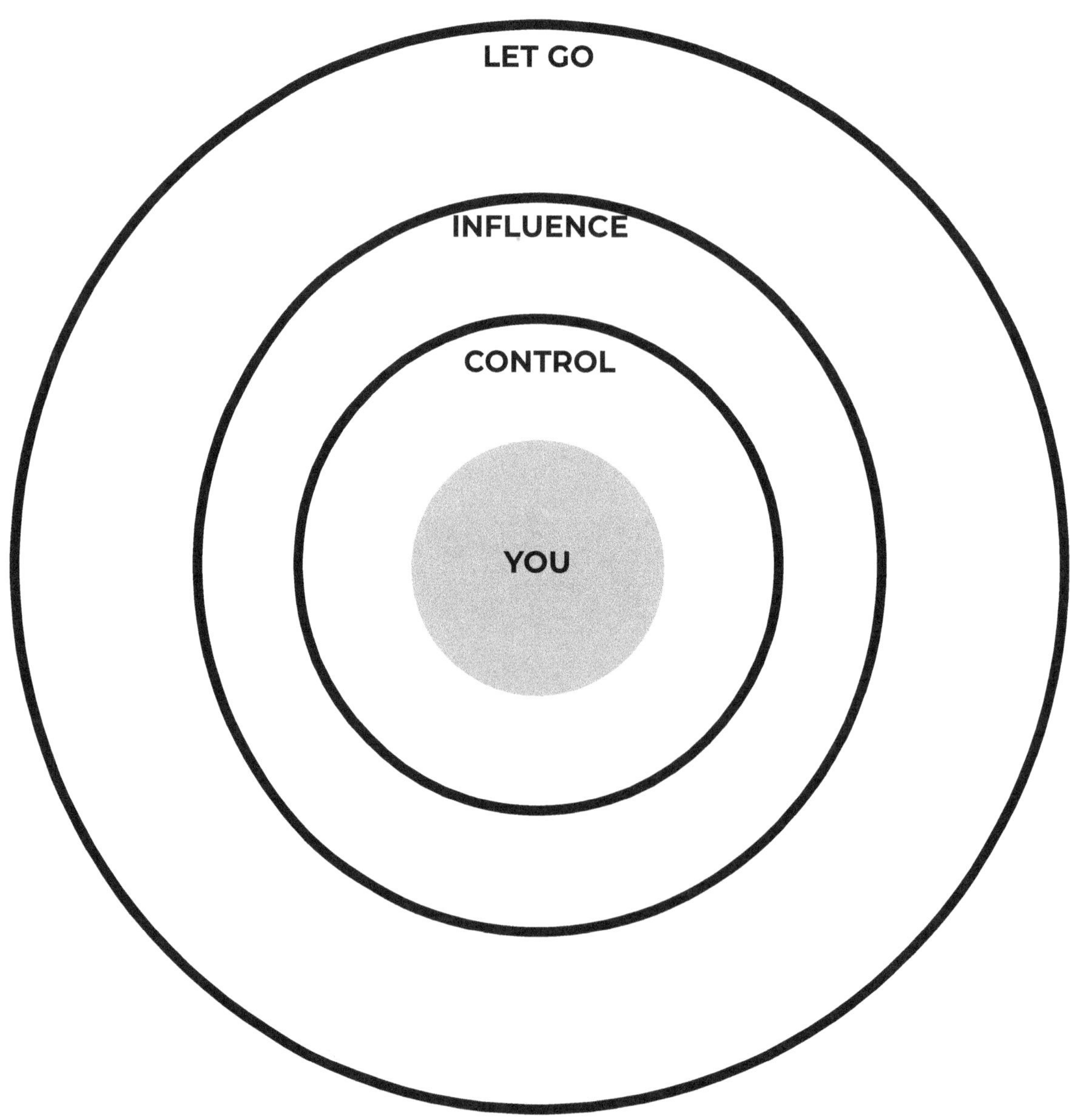

5 - The View at 34,000 ft.

It's winter. You're in the middle of your days off and feeling kind of bored. You look at the weekend forecast and see a cold snap coming. Desperate for some sunshine you consider non-revving to somewhere warm. However, it's peak season and your bank account is not in the mood for resort fees. Not willing to give up on your dream, you check open time to see if there are any easy trips that will bring you some warmth. You see a wonderful Caribbean layover. As an added bonus, you get to fly with a friend.

You rarely get to see this friend as they commute so their bid preferences usually don't match with yours. A year ago, you had a trip together, but they ended up calling out sick. You pick up the trip and start planning for your fun in the Sun. When you arrive at the airport for your trip, you notice your friend is no longer on the trip. You text them. They called out sick.

"What's wrong with you? You're always sick," you respond.

Your friend responds, "I haven't been sick since last year."

This chapter is about perception. Our reality is based off our unique perception. Only you have the ability to see the world through your eyes. Because we don't have the ability, nor the time, our perception of others is often built on the limited information provided with gaps filled in by our own experience, biases, and values. In other words, we see the world how we are.

Let's explore how we perceive others and therefore learn how others perceive us. Doing this will allow us to be more psychologically flexible, build empathy, and strengthen our self-compassion.

Filling in the Blanks

People are complex and diverse. We all carry multiple identities that influence how we perceive the world and how others perceive us. Examples of these identities include flight attendant, mother, husband, breast cancer survivor, musician, Christian, dog parent, gamer, and countless others.

Of course, we don't always have all our identities on display. We're entitled to privacy. On the other hand, some identities are always on display while on duty such as our occupation, gender, and race. While we have some control over how much information about ourselves we communicate, our minds tend to fill in the missing information based off our own experiences and biases. We can only work with the information we are given. To illustrate this concept, look at figure 5.1 below.

This is particularly true for flight attendants. During boarding, inflight crew only have a few crucial moments to determine if a passenger is fit to fly. An encyclopedia of experience in working with people is accessed in a matter of seconds to make these judgments.

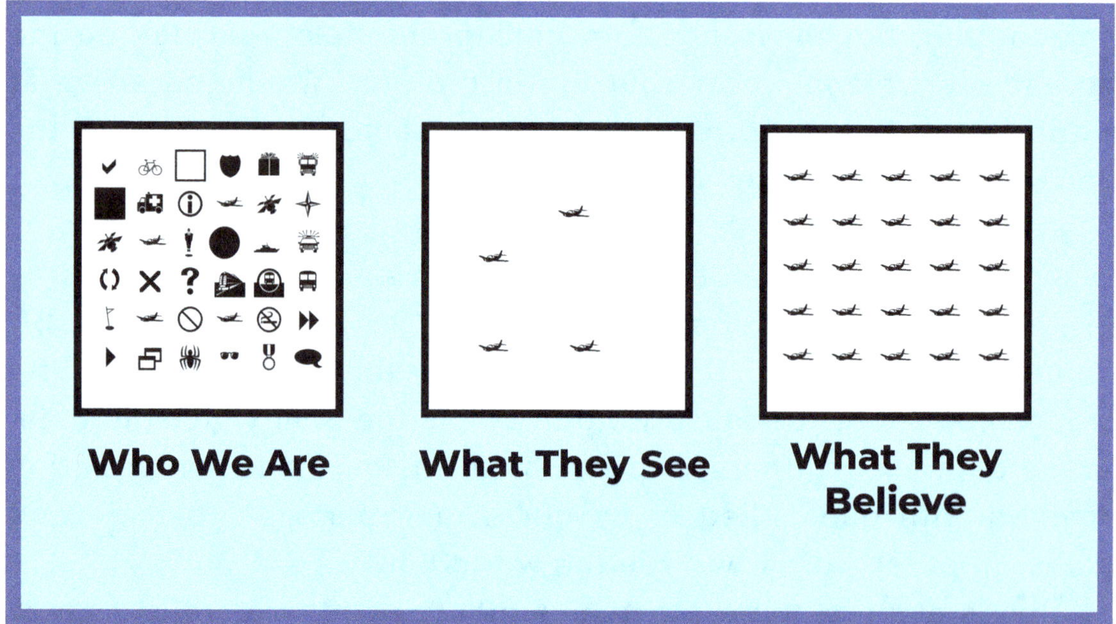

Figure 5.1

Exercise 5-A
Your Uniform and Luggage

Some identities we wear on the outside much like our uniform. Other identities we keep to ourselves until we feel comfortable enough to share them. Next to the flight attendant below, write the identities you display on duty on the left and the ones hidden on the right.

Exercise 5-B
Window Shade Open or Closed?

We can manage how others perceive us by deciding what information to disclose. Usually, we gauge this by the level of intimacy in our relationships or based on the setting. Picture an aircraft cabin window. The sunshine on the outside of the aircraft is information about us. We can decide how much light we want in. If we find someone is "in the dark" about us, we can open the shade a little to provide more light.

Fill out the window shades below to determine what information you would like to share in various situations. Write what you would like to keep private on the shade and what you are okay with being public on the window.

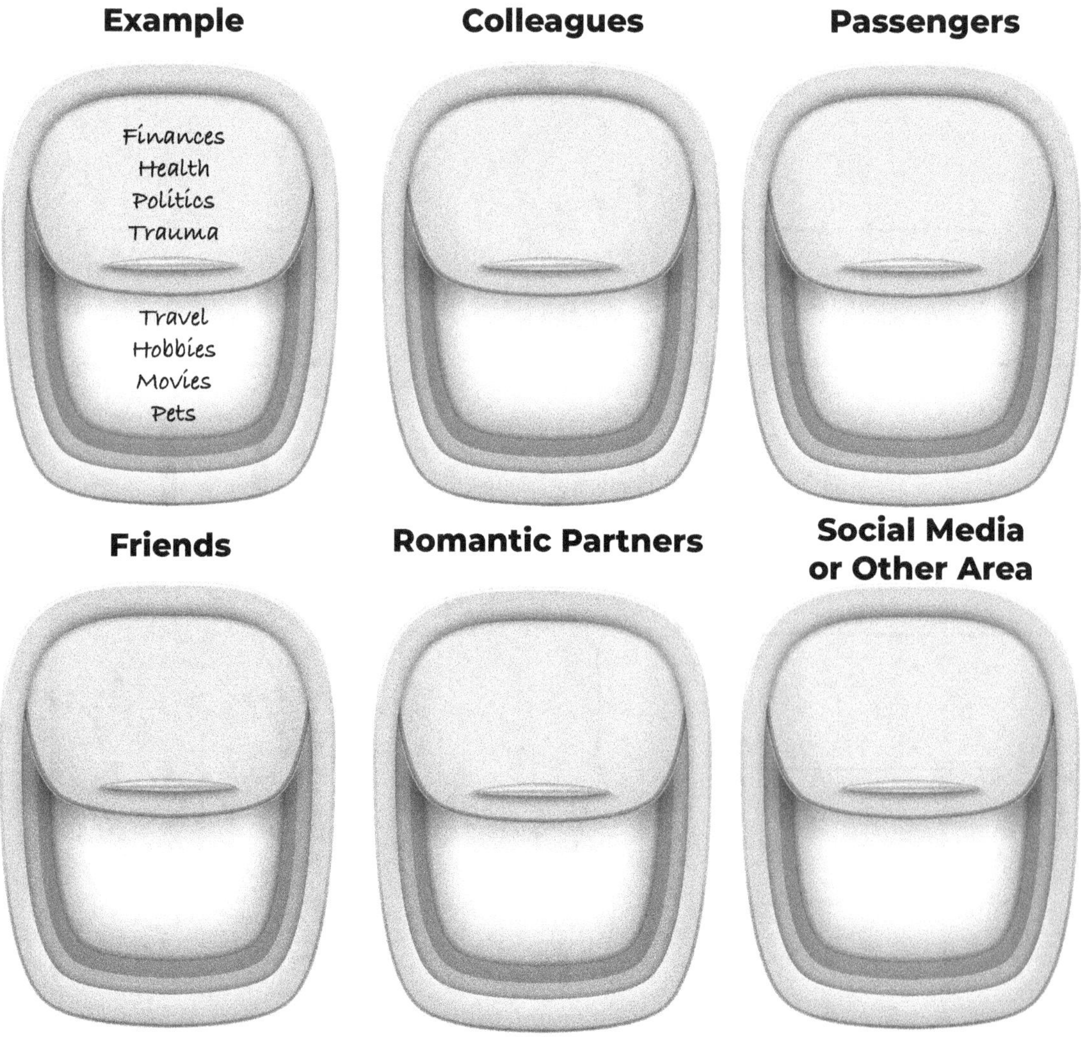

Why Give More Information?

It may be difficult to understand why we would want to give more information to others we do not know. As explained earlier, our perceptions are based off the information we have. Since our perceptions shape reality, we may need to provide more information if someone's perception is causing distress.

Imagine you are working a short haul flight. The boarding began on time but because the flight was only half-full, boarding completed 15 minutes before departure. A passenger with limited travel experience or anxiety may begin to wonder why the plane is still at the gate. Five minutes before departure, two more passengers board and the door closes. You push off the gate 3 minutes early and are on your way.

A week later, you are reviewing passenger feedback and notice a passenger on that flight complained that the flight was late because of the wait for two passengers. You review the information and see that the flight left and arrived early. Now your net promoter score is down because this passenger perceived a delay. One way to mitigate this in the future is to let passengers know that boarding completed early so there will be a brief hold at the gate for departure time. More information can change someone's reality.

Flight attendants on reserve are usually aware of this effect as they may be covering a delayed flight for lack of crew. Letting the passengers know that you are a last-minute replacement can deflect passenger ire and even make you appear heroic.

Exercise 5-C
Guess The Passenger

Match the passenger to the list of careers below.

____

____

Career List

School Teacher	Chef
Software Engineer	Nurse
Real Estate Developer	Account Executive

Portraits AI Generated With Adobe Firefly

Exercise 5-D
Now Boarding

YuriArcursPeopleImages/envatoelements

These are the passengers boarding your flight. Study their faces for only a few seconds each, or as much time as you would get during boarding.

Put a circle around the passenger you believe will be the nicest.
Put an X across the passenger you believe will be irritable.
Put a star on the passenger you could see being friends with.
Put a triangle on the passenger that reminds you of someone with whom you've had a bad experience (I.E.: an ex, a bully, former passenger, colleague, family member).

Safety Briefing on Bias

If you found Exercise 5-C & D to be difficult, if not impossible, congratulations. If you found the exercises easy, that's okay, too. There were no right or wrong answers to these exercises. These exercises were designed to provoke the implicit bias we all carry. Implicit means that it is hidden and often we are unaware.

Implicit biases develop based on a variety of factors such as life experience, societal factors, the media, and upbringing. To illustrate, if the majority of your interactions with difficult passengers involve businessmen, you may be more apprehensive before interacting with passengers who are businessmen. Or, if a passenger reminds you of an ex that broke your heart, you may have a negative feeling towards a passenger that reminds you of your ex.

These reactions are natural as our brain is working with the information we have. To work within this framework, we simply need to acknowledge that these biases do exist, they may be at play when having strong reactions to someone, and we are open to adjusting our viewpoints in light of this information. Being willing to change our perception and accept that our assumptions could be wrong is a huge step in combating behaviors triggered by implicit bias. As you recall in Chapter 4, it's not the thought that matters but what we do after.

It's also wise to use this perspective when considering why we don't like working certain routes. Reflect back to a when you worked a flight to a dreaded destination, and you encountered passengers stereotypical of that route. How many were actually behaving that way? Are we letting a handful of passengers ruin our entire flight?

You can learn more about your implicit bias by taking a test at http://implicit.harvard.edu.

Exercise 5-E
Where Did That Come From?

Review your answers for Exercise 5-D. Look at the passengers you marked with an X and a triangle. Let's explore your answers.

> **What about the X passenger made you anticipate their irritability? If you need to, share a story from your past that brought you to this conclusion.**

> **What about the triangle passenger reminded you of a difficult person from your past? How likely is it this person will behave in the same manner?**

Exercise 5-F
Oopps... I Was Wrong Again

Initial assumptions can often be wrong. Use the blanks below to reflect on the following situations.

Think about a time when a passenger or co-worker made an incorrect assumption about you. What was it? How did you feel? What information were they missing?

Think about a time when you made an incorrect assumption about a passenger or co-worker. What was it? How did you feel being wrong? What information were you missing?

Remember, it's okay to be wrong if we're willing to learn.

Exercise 5-G
Present Moment Checklist

It's been a few pages since we've intentionally engaged with the present moment. Use this checklist whenever you are feeling disconnected and dwelling on the past or future.

Breathing: Fully and deeply into the abdomen

Tension: Where am I feeling tension in my body?

Emotion: Acknowledge the emotion experienced.

Thoughts: Does this need my immediate attention?

Urges: What are they telling me to do?

Perspective: Am I missing information?

Psychic: Am I using the past to predict the future?

Exercise 5-H
Sky Writing

evanat/EnvatoElements

Write a story about the above graphic:

If you included any emotion words, write them here:

6 - Holding Patterns

DC_Studio/EnvatoElements

After a long duty day, you decide to join your crew in the hotel bar for debriefing and bonding over drinks. While you get to know each other, the conversation continually circles back to work. It makes sense because that's what brought you all together. A colleague brings up the new uniforms in testing. Everyone at the table has something critical to say about the new uniforms, except you.

A couple glasses of wine in, you say, "I actually like the uniforms."

Everyone at the table laughs. Some playfully tease you about your opinion by calling you a company man. Other try to convince you that you are wrong. Before long, the night ends. You have an early van time tomorrow.

The next morning, you meet your crew on the shuttle to the airport. You say good morning. No one responds. You start to wonder if you're being excluded for expressing your opinion on the new uniforms. For the flight home, you keep to yourself and only speak to your colleagues about things pertinent to the flight. You believe they don't like you and add them to your "no fly list" after landing.

As you read in the previous chapter, our minds will fill in the blanks if we don't have all the information. Sometimes, our minds engage in cognitive distortions which are like thinking holding patterns. Much like how an airplane can be delayed by a holding pat-

-tern, our happiness and life satisfaction can be delayed if we engage in these thinking traps too often.

In this chapter, we will review these common thinking holding patterns, how to recognize them, and how to move on from them.

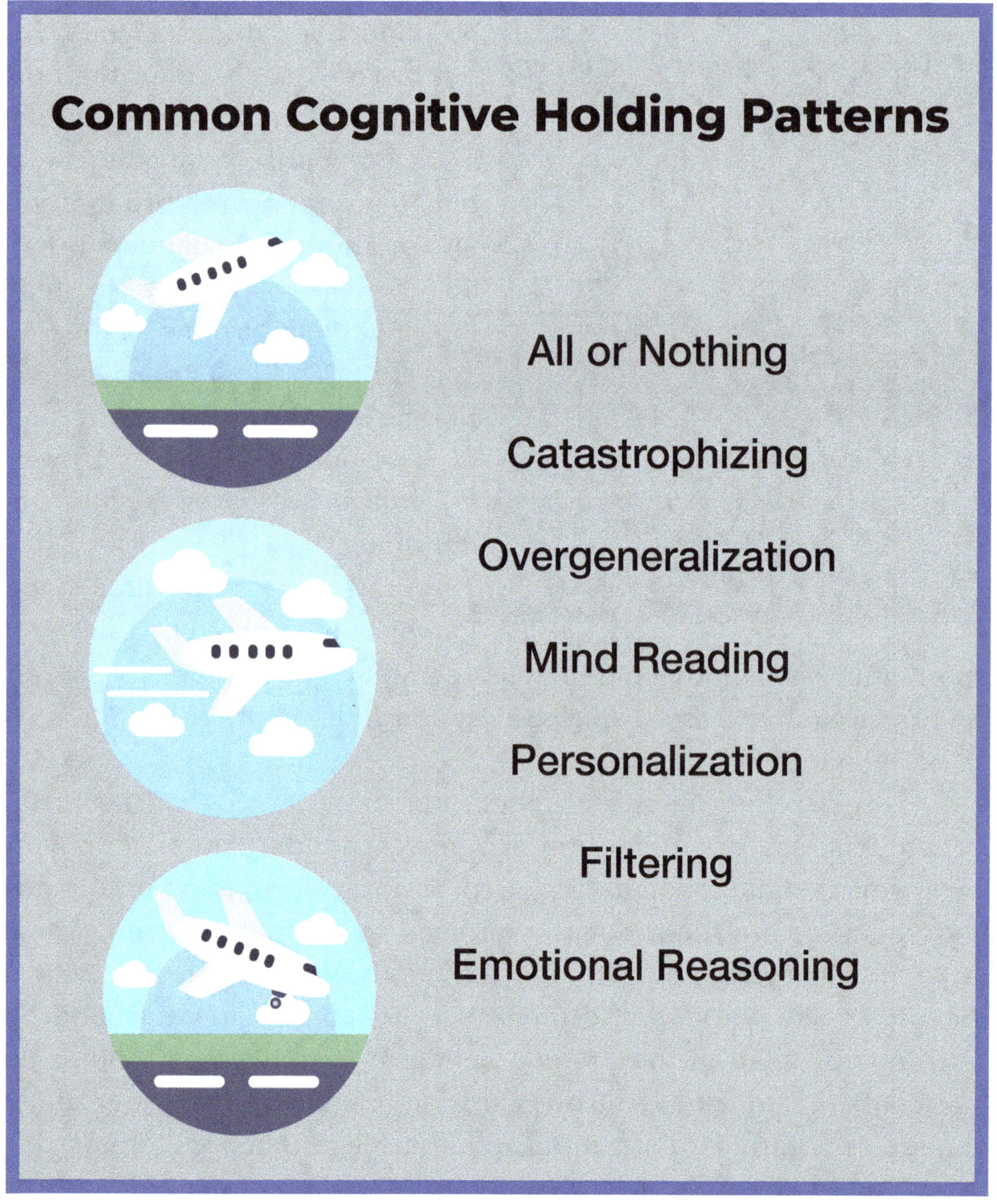

thedighital/EnvatoElements

All or Nothing Thinking

All or Nothing thinking is looking at events, people, concepts, and the world in general as either black or white. Reality is more complex and operates in shades of grey.

Perfect Service or Complete Failure

As a purser, you meticulously planned a service for passengers, aiming for a flawless experience. However, a minor hiccup occurs – catering forgot to load cloth napkins. In the realm of all-or-nothing thinking, you might perceive the entire service as a complete failure because it didn't meet the unrealistic expectation of perfection.

Consequences of All or Nothing Thinking

- Feeling a deep sense of failure and disappointment.
- The positive aspects of the experience are overshadowed.
- Overall job satisfaction may be affected as you tie your success to an unattainable standard of perfection.

Reality Check

Evaluate the situation more holistically. Instead of viewing it as either perfect or a failure, recognize the positive elements. Acknowledge that small imperfections are a normal part of any service industry, and focus on improvement rather than aiming for unattainable perfection.

Provide an example of all or nothing thinking:

Catastrophizing

Catastrophizing is when we only see the worst possible outcome of a situation.

I'm Going to be Fired

Your inflight manager sends you an e-mail requesting a meeting before your next trip. Despite not knowing what the meeting is about, you believe you will be terminated. You begin to wonder how you will pay your rent or what you will do for work.

Consequences of Catastrophizing

- Extreme anxiety or panic.
- Unnecessary preparations.

Reality Check

Negativity bias and imagining the worst case scenario are ways our mind tries to prepare us for survival. Thank your mind for protecting you and then remember there is also a best case scenario. Once you've established the best case scenario, imagine the countless possibilities in between that are all just as likely.

Another way to combat catastrophizing is to write out the worst case scenario. Don't hold anything back. Make it absolutely tragic. Read it outloud. How realistic does it sound?

Provide an example of catastrophizing:

Overgeneralization

Overgeneralization is when we make broad interpretations based off of a few events.

Always Late!

You experience a delayed departure on one flight due to unforeseen circumstances. Overgeneralization leads you to believe that this delay is indicative of a pattern, assuming that all future flights will also be late. You may develop a belief that punctuality is unachievable, affecting your outlook on future flights.

Consequences of Overgeneralization

- Expecting every similar situation will have the same outcome because of your recent experience.
- Increased stress and frustration.
- Not fully appreciating situations where things go smoothly as they are overshadowed by negative events.

Reality Check

Combat the generalization by recalling similar situations in which things did work out. Embrace negative situations as challenges and opportunities to learn. Ask yourself, is it realistic to expect things to go according to plan 100% of the time?

Provide an example of overgeneraliztion:

Mind Reading

Mind Reading is when we make assumptions about other's thoughts or motivations without adequate evidence.

They Hate Me

You observe a passenger with a seemingly serious facial expression and immediately concludes that the passenger is dissatisfied or upset. You engage in mind reading by assuming you know what the passenger is thinking or feeling without direct communication.

Consequences of Mind Reading

- Negative interactions with others as we assume how they feel.
- A diminished sense of self.
- The other person feeling misunderstood.

Reality Check

Does this person have a reason to be upset with you? Did this person verbally communicate their feelings with you?

Personalization

Personalization is when we feel responsible for events beyond our control.

Airport Operations

After a long flight, you arrive at your destination. Due to a lack of gate space, your aircraft is parked at a remote stand. Stairs are used to deplane the passengers. Several passengers require wheelchair assistance and will be delayed while the proper equipment is pro-cured. While you apologize on behalf of the company for the delay, deep down you feel like there was something you could have done to prevent this situation.

Consequences of Personalization

- Feelings of guilt or shame.
- Believing you will face consequences for this situation.
- Additional occupational stress when faced with similar situations.

Reality Check

Evaluate your role in the situation and consider external factors. Remember that we function as a team. Revisit Exercise 4-G to deter-mine what you can and cannot control.

Provide an example of personalization:

Filtering (Selective Abstraction)

Filtering is when we focus on one piece of information instead of considering all of the evidence.

Passenger Surveys

Suppose your airline sends out satisfaction surveys after every flight. You get to access a report with all the results. The majority of the results were positive. However, there was one passenger complaint. You believe you are bad at your job because of one complaint.

Consequences of Filtering

- Unnecessary self-doubt and diminished sense of accomplishment.
- The positive aspects are overshadowed by the negative.
- Your confidence and job satisfaction begin to erode.

Reality Check

Look at the full spectrum of data available to you. Why are you letting one piece of information determine your worth?

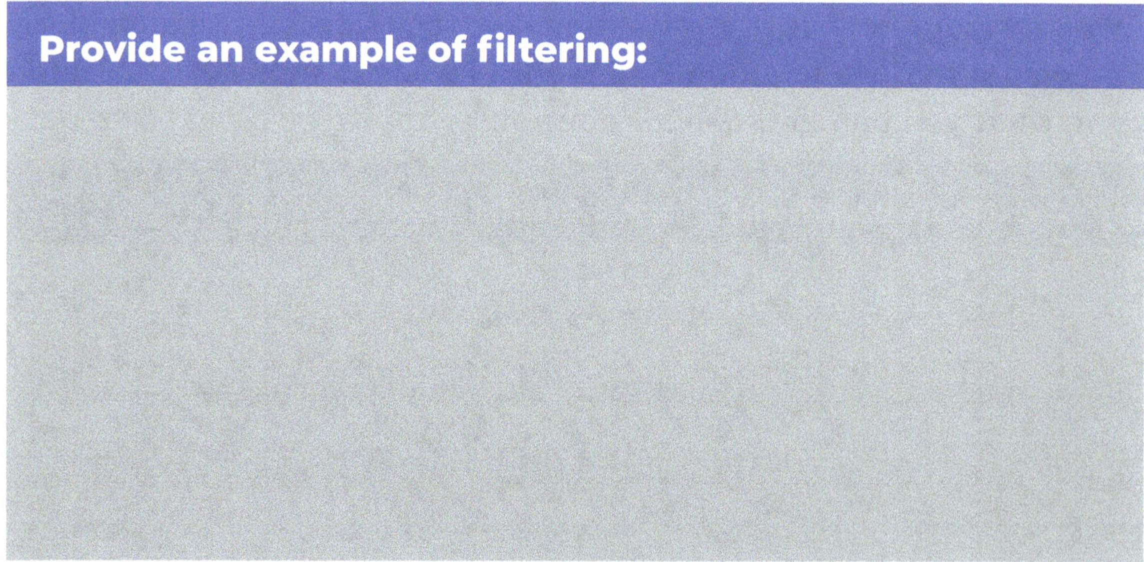

Emotional Reasoning

Emotional Reasoning is when we assume our emotions reflect reality.

Galley Feedback

After working the business class galley for the first time, you receives constructive criticism from the purser about a specific aspect of the service. Instead of objectively considering the feedback, you emotionally reason that because you feel hurt or upset, the criticism must signify a personal failure.

Consequences of Emotional Reasoning

- Heightened emotional distress.
- Misunderstanding with others.
- Poor decision making.

Reality Check

Consider all of the evidence. Is the emotion you are feeling congruent to the situation? If not, what else could be bothering you?

Provide an example of emotional reasoning:

Exercise 6-A
Banner Tow

Read each banner and decide whether the thought is a holding pattern by checking the box.

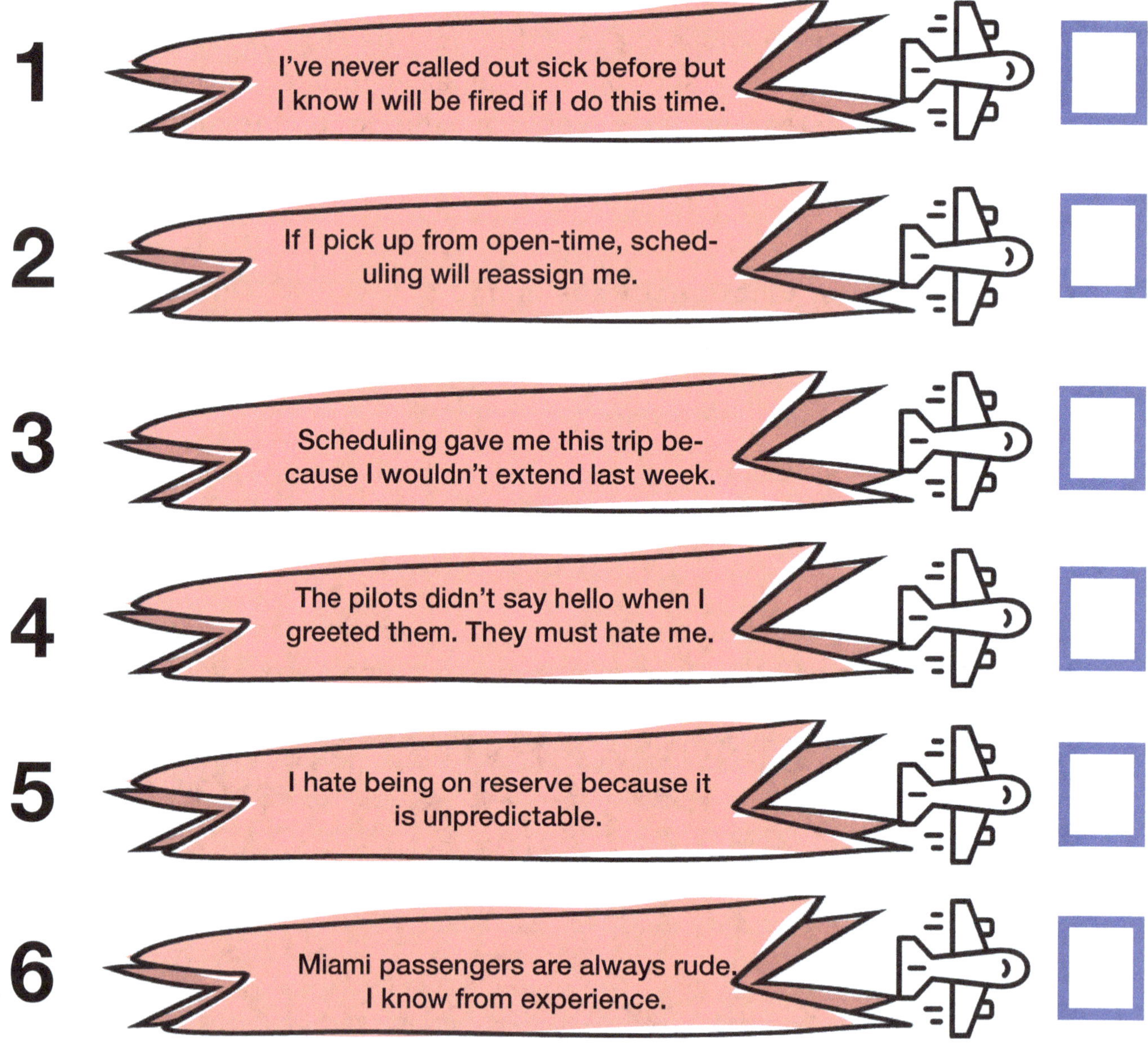

Answer Key: 1:Y, 2:Y, 3:Y, 4:Y, 5:N, 6:Y

Cleared to Land

As you can see, many of these cognitive holding patterns are very similar. Analyzing the information available to you and comparing it to your beliefs can assist you in breaking out of the holding pattern for a smooth landing. The exercise below is a classic analysis technique used in Cognitive Behavioral Therapy. A blank worksheet is provided on the next page.

Exercise 6-B
ABC Analysis (Example)

A - Activating Event

Spilled a glass of wine on a passenger during beverage service. Even though I apologized, the passenger was very upset and said she was going to share her experience on social media.

B - Belief (Is this a holding pattern?)

I'm going to get fired. I'm going to have to move back in with my parents because I don't know what else I can do for work.

C - Consequence/Emotion

Depressed and anxious. I couldn't sleep during my layover thinking about the complaint this passenger will send in.

Evidence For	Evidence Against
She seemed very upset. She stated her blouse was very expensive and I ruined her trip.	Accidents happen. I've never had a passenger complaint before. My crew backed me up.

Exercise 6-B
ABC Analysis

A - Activating Event

B - Belief (Is this a holding pattern?)

C - Consequence/Emotion

Evidence For

Evidence Against

7 - Lost Signals

Imagine you're returning home from a long-haul flight. You started your day halfway around the world while everyone back home was still sleeping. After serving three meals, countless drinks, and picking up tons of trash, you are ready for your days off. Before you left on your trip, you cleaned your apartment and stocked the refrigerator. All you want to do is cocoon for the next 12 hours while you decompress.

Upon entering your home, you notice a few things out of place. Your partner isn't the tidiest of people, but it's nice to come home to a familiar face. Walking to your bedroom, you pass by the kitchen. The sink is full of dishes. Shaking your head in disappointment you turn towards your room and see an unmade bed. You let out a sigh. You've told your partner that you like to return from a trip to a clean apartment, but he doesn't seem to listen. You begin to wonder if moving in together was a bad idea.

MariaSiurt/EnvatoElements

This chapter is about communication both on and off the plane. The exercises in this chapter will help you to be able to advocate your needs effectively, shape behavior, keep it cool during conflict, and become a better listener.

Effective communication is the foundation of successful interactions, fostering understanding and collaboration while minimizing misunderstandings. Clear and concise communication empowers individuals to express ideas, share feedback, and navigate challenges confidently, creating a supportive environment where ideas flourish and relationships thrive.

Exercise 7-A
Social Signaling

Imagine you arrived at your layover hotel. After putting down your luggage, you decide to take a shower to freshen up after a long day of flying. As the shower runs, you realize the drain is backed up. You try calling the front desk, but no one is picking up. Realizing you would rather just have a new room, you decide to pack everything up and request a new room in person. At the front desk you notice four associates.

AI Generated Images by Adobe Firefly

Being aware of our facial expressions and body language when communicating can yield to more positive interactions with others whether we are on the giving or receiving end of a request. Facial expressions can carry additional context to communication that words alone cannot achieve. We can also influence another person's mood through facial expressions. To test this out, smile at someone and see if they smile back.

Additional social safety signals to use when communicating include eyebrow wags, nodding, relaxed arms, eye contact, and turning your body towards the person you are communicating with. How does it feel when you are chatting with a friend, and they are looking at their phone instead of looking at you?

I Versus You Statements

Another technique when communicating is to use "I" statements rather than "you" statements. In chapter 5, we discussed how we can only see things through our perspective. When sharing our observations or judgments with others, it's important to frame it from our perspective. This shows that we are open to new information from their perspective and doesn't feel like an attack on the receiver.

Here are some examples to show you how to reframe "you" statements to "I" statements. You can practice on the next page.

You never fly domestic.

I feel like you don't ever fly domestic.

You need to put on your seatbelt.

I've noticed your seatbelt is not on. Can you buckle it for me?

You're always sick.

I feel like every time we talk you are sick.

You are making me angry.

I'm feeling upset.

You never pay attention to me.

I would like if you paid a more attention to me.

Exercise 7-B
It's Not You, It's Me

Rewrite the following statements from your perspective.

You're always late.

You're not listening to me.

You don't care about me.

You take things too seriously.

You're always looking at your phone.

You are irritating me.

You never help with the kids.

Exercise 7-C
What's Your Destination?

Now we need to establish what we want from an interaction. Entering a conversation with our goals in mind can keep us focused on what's important to us and prevent us from getting lost in distractions, tangents, or side-quests. Use the worksheet below to clarify your communication goals.

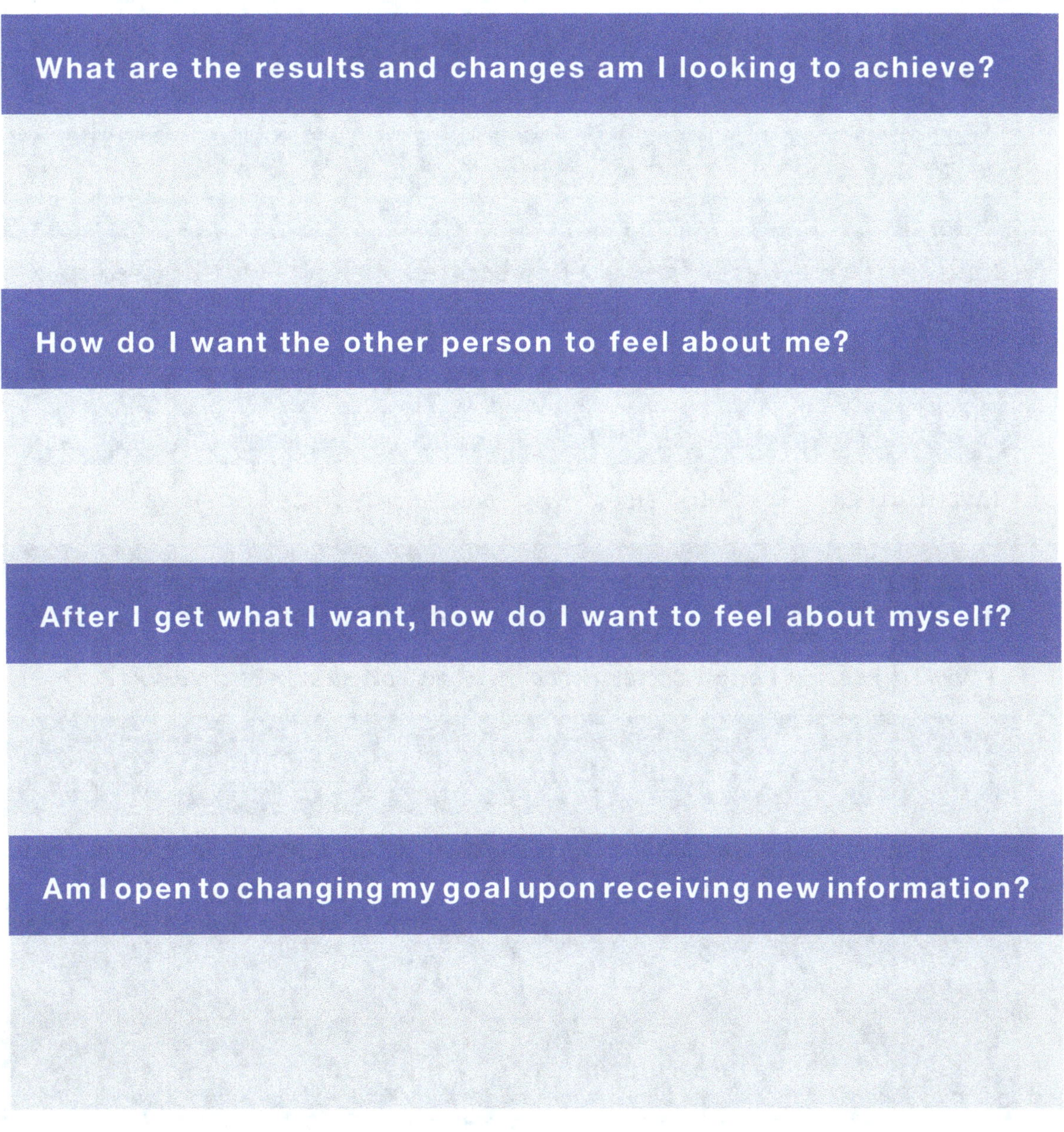

Dear Man

This direct communication technique was developed by Marsha M. Linehan (2015), developer for Dialectical Behavioral Therapy or DBT. DBT offers many interpersonal effectiveness techniques to apply in your daily life. Check out the example below and the use Exercise 7-D to practice on your own.

D - Describe the situation using only the facts:

I noticed all the groceries that I bought before my trip were gone by the time I returned home.

E - Express your feelings/opinions from your perspective:

I buy my groceries before my trip because I know I will be tired and hungry when I return.

A - Assert. Here is where you ask for what you want:

I would like you to buy your own food to eat while I'm gone.

R - Reinforce. Here is where you describe the consequences:

I would be in a much better mood and much easier to deal with.

M - Mindful. How will you ignore attacks and distractions?

Yes, I know I left the bathroom a mess. I'll try harder. But, right now we are talking about the groceries.

A - Appear effective and confident.

N - Negotiate. Are you willing to adjust your request? How?

You can eat it as long as you replace it before I return.

Exercise 7-D
Dear Man Practice

The final direct communication technique we will reveal was developed by Marsha M. Linehan (2015), developer for Dialectical Behavioral Therapy or DBT. DBT offers many interpersonal effectiveness techniques to apply in your daily life.

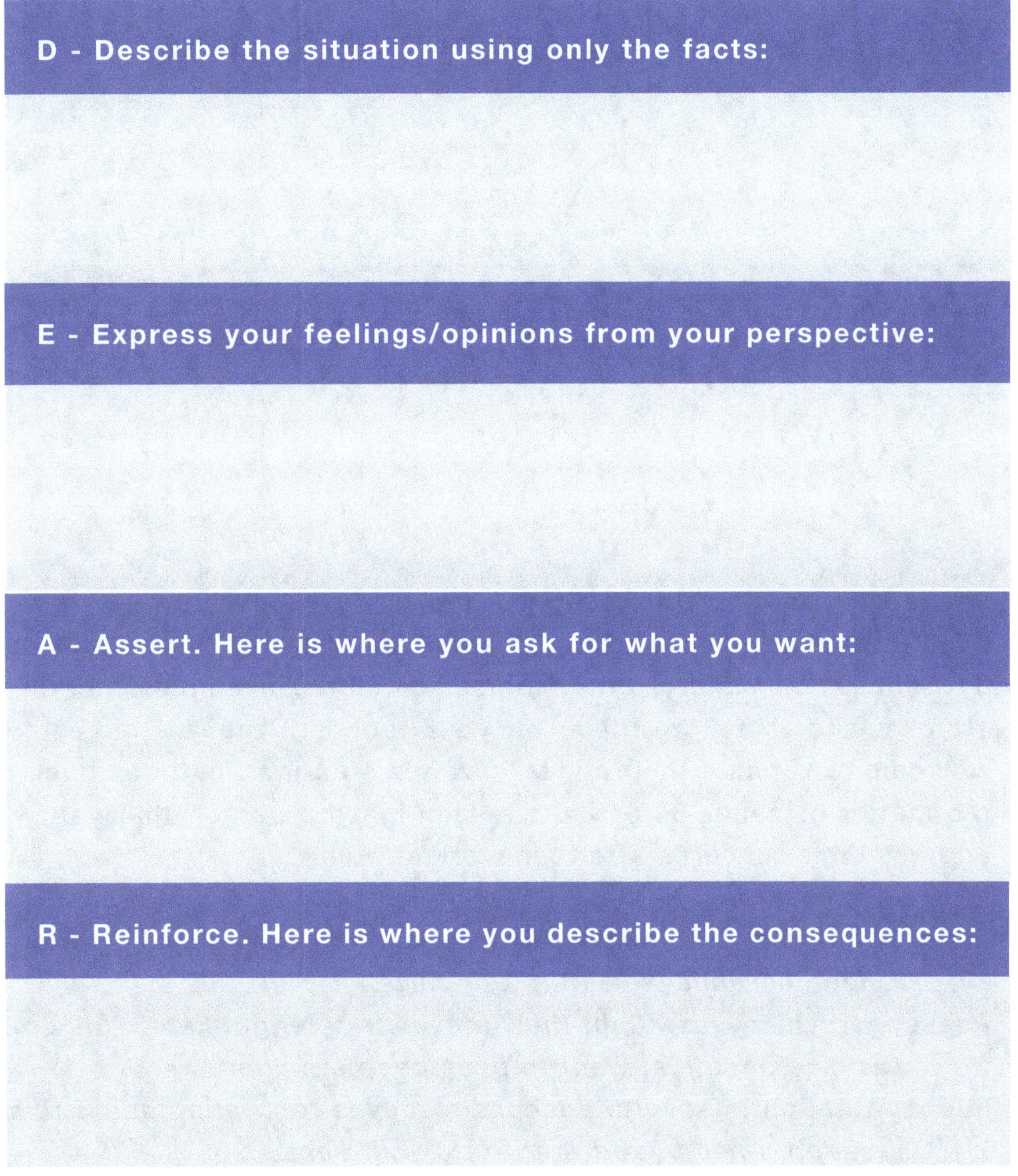

M - Mindful. How will you ignore attacks and distractions?

A - Appear. How will you appear effective and competent?

N - Negotiate. Are you willing to adjust your request? How?

Staying focused on the task at hand is key especially in difficult situations. It is common for someone to put you on the defensive by bringing up history, other topics, unrelated examples, personal attacks, and more pushback on your request. You are more than welcome to validate their concerns while steering the focus back to the matter at hand. Sometimes reassuring the person that you will address their concerns after can work as well.

Flight Attendant: *I cannot have you stretch in the galley. It is too dangerous while we set up our carts.*
Passenger: *On my last flight they let me stretch right here. That crew was nicer. You just want to boss people around.*
Flight Attendant: *I know the inconsistency is frustrating but in this situation, I need you to return to your seat.*

Exercise 7-E
Praise Be

We all like to know when we are doing something that pleases others. Praise can encourage us to continue a certain behavior and possibly influence others who witness the praise.

Describe a situation in which you were thanked at work:

How did it feel to receive that acknowledgement?

Did the praise influence your future behavior?

Try it: The next time you are boarding an aircraft. Thank a passenger individually for performing a pro-social behavior such as stowing bags properly, putting a tray table up, or moving out of the aisle to let crew through. If a passenger complies with your request, be sure to praise them. "Thank you for returning to your seat."

When Things Go Wrong

Because we all have unique perspectives, different experiences, distinct values, and competing motivations, conflicts are inevitable. Disagreements can be challenging. Our ancestors learned that cooperation was key to survival. Being ostracized from one's tribe was a death sentence.

Conflicts and disagreements with others can tap into these primitive aversions to rejection and exclusion as our brain sees conflict as a threat to survival. In the process, our brain switches into survival mode (also known as fight, flight,

Pressmaster/EnvatoElements

or freeze). In this mode, our mind is shut off to reasoning. Emotions control the show.

Being the social animals that we are, it is easy for others to also switch into survival mode when around someone in that state. If we feel we are not understood while in distress, we may get louder or engage in more extreme behavior to get our point across or to get others to join us. Social media is full of videos where simple situations escalate quickly into loud disagreements because someone didn't feel heard.

It is important to be mindful of this human process when interacting with those in distressed states. It is very easy to join them by matching their emotions or aggression. Remember that these people are in survival mode, and they need to be brought back to a safe space before reasoning can happen. In the next chapter we will examine distress tolerance techniques that you can model for others.

For the purposes of effective communication, when we verbally reflect the core emotion behind distressed communication, we let the other person know they are heard. Being heard minimizes feelings of rejection which bring the person out of survival mode. The next exercise will help you fine tune that skill.

Reflections

Reflections are a communication skill we can employ to signal to someone that we hear them and understand them. People who feel listened to are less likely to feel distressed and less likely to escalate unwanted behaviors. We can reflect the content of someone's message by paraphrasing what is being said and labelling an emotion. As you practice this skill more and more, start looking for the deeper meaning hidden in their message. Most people know the solutions to their problem are limited and will be more receptive to problem solving once they feel they've been heard.

> **When you're gone for work, it is so hard to keep up with the household tasks while watching the kids and going to work.**

It sounds like you appreciate when I'm around and would like some help with responsibilities while I'm traveling.

> **Every time I fly your airline, we're late. I end up missing meetings which could jeopardize my business deals.**

It must be frustrating to not be able to rely on the times printed on your boarding pass. Is there anything I can do right now?

> **I am not splitting my family up. We purchased these seats together, we are sitting together.**

It sounds like you really enjoy spending time with your family.

Exercise 7-F
Reflections Practice

Now it's your turn. Read the following statements and respond by reflecting the content and emotion. Bonus points if you can reflect back the deeper meaning.

PS: We can always check-in to see if our reflection is accurate by asking, "Did I get that right?"

> **You never message me when you land so that I know you arrived safely.**

> **We're always hanging out with your friends but we never hang out with my friends.**

> **When you come home from a trip, you never want to do anything. All you want to do is sleep.**

Misconnect

Would you rather a take direct flight or make a connection? Just like a direct flight will get you to your destination faster than connecting, direct communication can help you achieve your goals faster. However, indirect communication is often chosen as

thananit_s/EnvatoElements

it can be perceived as more polite. In many cases, this is true.

Flight attendants are experts at calibrating communication through situational awareness. However, there are times we may misuse indirect communication to avoid responsibility, hide intentions, and disguise demands in a way that escalates the situation. The expression, "Don't shoot the messenger" comes to mind.

An example of indirect communication that can escalate a situation is asking questions that we already know the answer to. Using the vignette at the start of this chapter as an example, imagine if the flight attendant saw that their bed was not made and then proceeded to ask their partner, "Did you make the bed?" The flight attendant already knows the answer to the question. So, what is the purpose of asking such a question?

Indirect communication is often a way for us to control a situation. By asking their partner this question, they are triggering feelings of shame or embarrassment as a way to humiliate or punish their partner. If the partner realizes this and calls out the foul play, the flight attendant has enough plausible deniability by responding, "I was just asking a question."

When deciding to engage in indirect communication, it is important to determine what are our intentions. Mindful awareness of our intentions can help us say what we mean without unnecessary emotional escalation.

Exercise 7-G
Reconnect (Say What You Mean)

Review the list of common indirect phrases that may be misinterpreted by the receiver. Write in an alternative, more direct phrase.

Indirect Phrase	Say What You Mean
Not Exactly	No / That's Wrong / Incorrect
Probably	
Maybe	
Not Bad	
Yes, but...	
Not right now.	
It's a possibility	
We'll see.	

8 - Returning to Base

You're in the middle of a busy business class meal service to Europe. The flight is full, and most of the passengers are traveling for leisure. On top of this, you're short a flight attendant. Every time you run an entrée, you have to stop and refill bread and wine. It slows

DC_Studio/EnvatoElements

down the service. You hear a chime. BING-BONG. You know it's the pilots asking about their meals.

"We're busy right now!" you answer the phone exasperated. "Call back later."

Before the captain can say anything, you hang up. After the service is over, you replay the interaction in your head. You feel bad. That outburst was out of character for you. You normally don't lose your cool under pressure; but this time, you were at the end of your rope.

Flight attendants are trained to keep their cool under the most extreme conditions. But no human is infallible. Occasionally, we have a reaction that's atypical for us.

This chapter is about distress tolerance. People in the service industry are habituated into keeping their emotions in check. But what happens when we experience too much stress? We've all read stories of flight attendants reaching the end of their composure and having an outburst; most notably the JetBlue flight attendant that blew a slide and quit.

Imagine you are a soda bottle. If you're calm, you can open up and express your effervescent self in a normal fashion. However, if you are continually shaken, you will explode when you are open. So how do we manage the pressure?

Emotional Leakage

We must learn to recognize when we need to release some pressure before it is too late. If we wait until we have an outburst, it may be the only thing people remember and we become known as emotionally unstable despite years of keeping it cool.

Think about how an aircraft is pressurized. Air comes in through the engines and is pressurized to match the air pressure at a more comfortable altitude. However, you cannot simply just keep adding pressurized air to the cabin as it will damage the structural integrity of the airframe. Therefore, various bleed points are designed into the aircraft to let the pressurized air out in a controlled fashion. Galley drains are one example of a bleed point. They utilize the pressure differential between the interior and exterior of the aircraft to suck liquid out of the aircraft.

nrradmin/EnvatoElements

In order to recognize if we are on the road to an outburst, we can take an inventory of our current emotional and physiological status. The Federal Aviation Administration (FAA) came up with a checklist for pilots to assess their wellbeing before each flight. The acronym is called IM SAFE. It stands for Illness, Medication, Stress, Alcohol, Fatigue, and Emotions.

In the next exercise, we've adapted the IM SAFE checklist to add additional factors that can affect our emotional wellbeing. By including food and recreation we create a holistic picture of you.

Exercise 8-A
IM SAFER Wellbeing Checklist

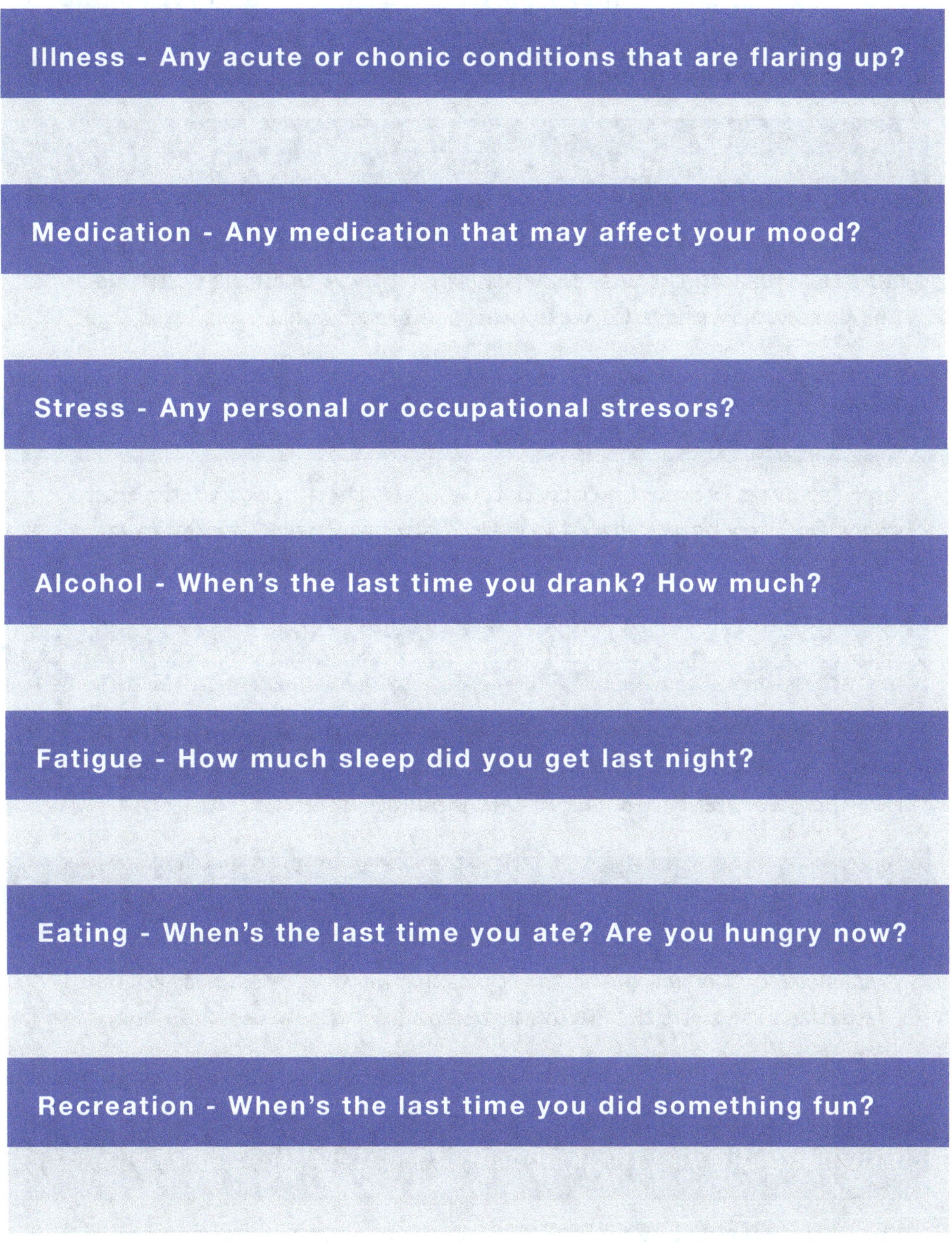

Exercise 8-B
My Signs of Stress (example)

Recall a situation in which you were so distressed that you acted out of character. Review the example below then fill out the event analysis on the next page to identify your physical signs of stress.

Describe The Situation:

A late arriving passenger couldn't find overhead space for their bags. I informed the passenger they will have to check their bag. The passenger refused and demanded closet space.

Were you able to focus or were your thoughts racing?

At first I was focused but their tone when they demanded closet space for their bags started my thoughts racing. Everyone was watching.

Describe your physical sensations (heart rate, breathing, etc)

Heart rate when up, tension in my jaw. Tingling in my hands and feet. Felt my vision narrowed (tunnel-vision). I don't remember my breathing but it was probably shallow.

What did you do? Did you regret it?

I responded. "Do you want to fly today, or not?" Yes, I regret it. I felt like I took out the "nuclear option" for a common on-board problem.

How long did you think about your interaction after the fact?

The entire flight. I avoided walking through economy so I could avoid interacting with the passenger.

Exercise 8-B
My Signs of Stress

Describe The Situation:

Were you able to focus or were your thoughts racing?

Describe your physical sensations (heart rate, breathing, etc)

What did you do? Did you regret it?

How long did you think about your interaction after the fact?

Keep note of the physical sensations you noticed. These are how your body signals distress to you.

Exercise 8-C
Quick Ways to Lower Distress

1. Let out a sigh.

2. Box Breathing (inhale 4, hold 4, exhale 4, hold 4, repeat).

3. Cold Shock - Place some ice on your forehead.

4. Squeeze - Find a stress ball or a pillow and squeeze it.

5. Count the number of passengers wearing glasses.

6. Try a strong mint to distract your brain.

7. Listen to a fun song and sing along if you can.

8. Step outside to get some fresh air.

9. Soothe yourself with your favorite warm beverage.

10. Look at photos of loved ones or pets on your phone.

11. Listen to a recording of nature sounds.

12. Smell calming essential oils such as lavender.

13. Talk it out. Phone a friend or trusted companion.

14. Carry something soft that you can rub your hands on.

15. Call on the higher power of your faith or meditate.

16. ____

Exercise 8-D
R.E.S.T. Before Reacting

As explained in chapter 7, when we are experiencing distress, our mind goes into survival mode. In these situations, it can be difficult to see the forest from the trees. As you begin to identify your unique signs of being distressed, you can use the space between realization and reaction to plan your response. Let's use the acronym R.E.S.T. to illustrate.

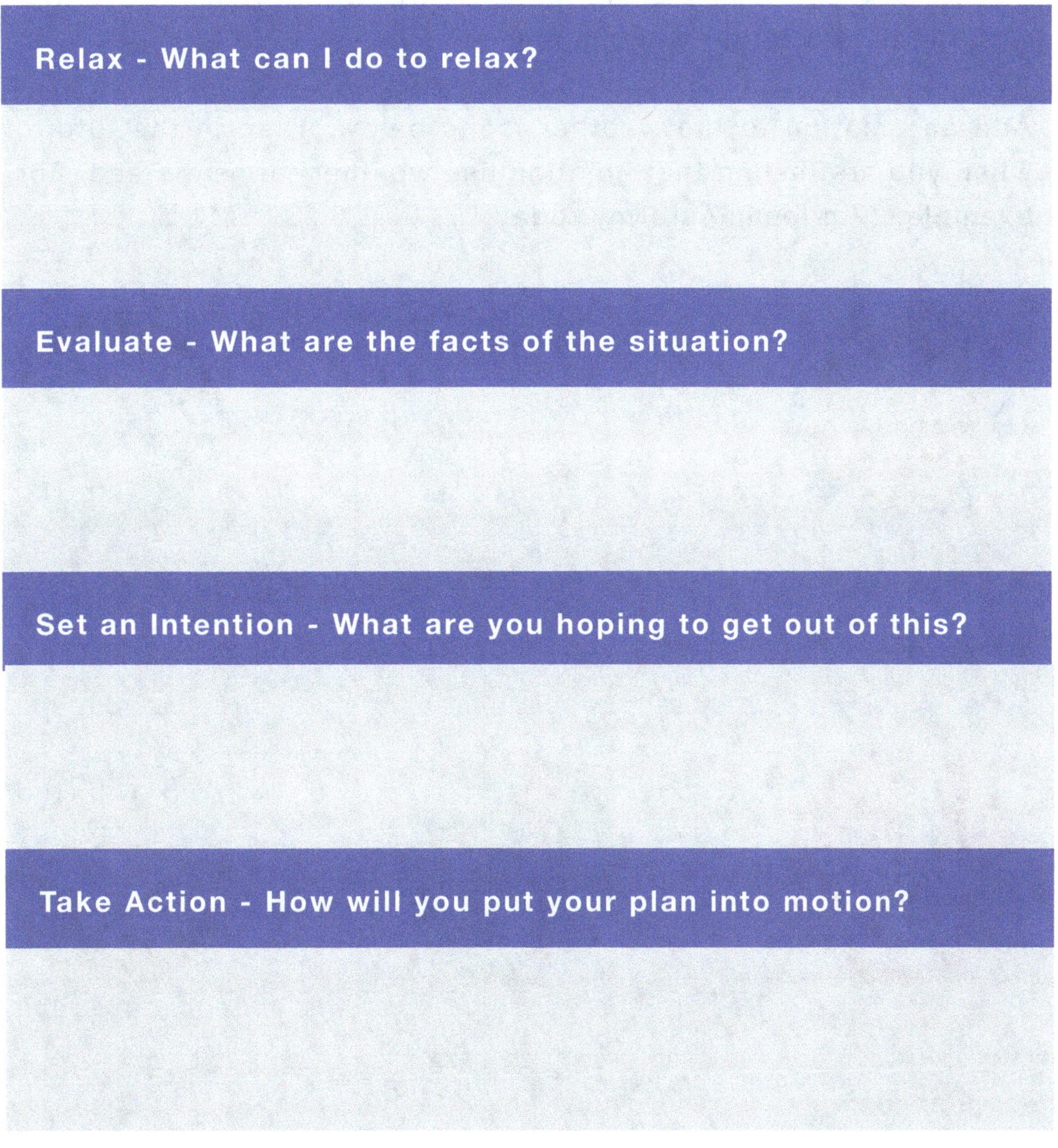

Exercise 8-E
Weather Forecast

Our minds dislike distress so much that we convince ourselves that our negative feelings are permanent in order to motivate us to change our current situation. Conversely, we rarely expect positive moments to last forever.

Imagine you are the sky, and your emotions are the weather. No matter how powerful the storm or cloudy the sky, we know that with time the weather will change.

Add an emotion to the weather icons below. Then in the future, when you are feeling that emotion use weather terms instead. For example, "I'm feeling stormy today."

Exercise 8-F
Passengers on the Plane

In the journey of life, imagine each of your thoughts and emotions as passengers on a plane. Some passengers are calm and pleasant, enjoying the in-flight entertainment. Others may be more anxious, causing a bit of disruption. The plane represents your mind,

VidEst/EnvatoElements

soaring through the skies of experiences and challenges. You are the pilot of this plane, navigating through the skies of your life. As the pilot, you have the ability to choose the direction and respond to various conditions.

Your life's challenges and distress are like turbulence you encounter enroute to your destination. Turbulence is a natural part of flight just like challenges are a natural part of life. You know that experiencing turbulent conditions does not jeopardize the safety of the flight.

The passengers, however, are unaware of this and begin to speak up every time the plane hits a bump. Some want the turbulence to stop, others want the plane to turn around, while others want to change the destination. It would be irrational to give in to these demands and changing the destination is like changing your goals. You also cannot force the passengers off the plane in the middle of the flight.

The goal in mindfulness is to acknowledge the passengers, even the challenging ones, while continuing to your destination. Mindfulness serves as the flight path, helping you stay present and attentive to the passengers and the journey. Mindful awareness allows you to observe the thoughts and emotions without being completely consumed by them.

Exercise 8-G
I'm Noticing... Am Aware Of

We can unhook ourselves from our emotions by taking a step back from them. By acknowledging our emotions, thoughts, and judgments out loud, we can separate ourselves from them allowing us to think before reacting.

Take a moment to tune into your mind. What is it saying?

1. Now say: "I am aware of..." or "I'm noticing..."

2. Now say: whether it is a thought, emotion, or sensation.

3. Label the thought, emotion, or sensation without explanation.

Let's put it all together. See the examples below:

I am aware of an emotion of frustration.

I am noticing a thought about inadequancy.

I am aware of an urge to quit my job.

I am noticing a sensation of tension in my jaw.

Exercise 8-H
Recognizing Triggers

Analyzing previous moments when you've felt triggered can help you recognize a react to a similar situation in the future. Fill out the analysis table below.

Stressor	Feelings	Thoughts	Behavior
Passenger said I skipped them during service but they were sleeping.	Frustration, annoyance.	I shouldn't have to apologize to people who aren't paying attention.	Tell the crew to watch out for that passenger.

Exercise 8-1
Recognizing Anger

Just like the thinking traps or holding patterns described in Chapter 6, anger can come with its own traps. Review the list of anger distortions below and provide an example form your life.

Blaming - Believing someone is responsible for your pain.

I would have held that trip if the out-of-base senior mamas didn't transfer here.

Magnifying - Exaggerating the impact of a situation.

It's absolutely terrible that they allow of bases to take our flying.

Global Labels - Painting someone as totally bad or good.

Everyone from that base is such a company kiss ass.

Misattributions - Jumping to conclusions and mind reading.

They only pick up our flying because they know it makes us mad.

Overgeneralization - Labeling events with "always" "never"

They should never allow out of base transfers to bid their seniority.

Commanding - Turning your personal preferences into law.

If I'm purser, I won't let an out of base flight attendant to run my galley.

Exercise 8-J
Does This Really Matter?

To close this chapter on distress, let's watch how our distress changes over time. Start this exercise when you encounter an intense emotion and continue with the sheet for the next week.

Describe the situation:

Name your emotion and rate it 0-10 (10 is most intense).

Rate how you think you will feel about this tomorrow 0-10.

Tomorrow: Rate your actual intensity of the emotion 0-10.

Next Week: Rate your actual intensity of the emotion 0-10.

Exercise 8-K
Only the Good Stuff

Our minds highlight the negative to help us learn from and avoid similar situations in the future. However, when we only remember the "bad stuff" we forget about the good things that happen. We may encounter one or two grumpy passengers per flight and start to view all passengers as adversarial. Use this log to counter negative encounters with positive ones.

Negative Encounter	Positive Encounter
Passenger blamed me for seat change.	Passenger complimented me on my earrings.

9 - Crossing Borders

You're working a 3-day domestic trip. It's very productive with barely any sit time and short layovers. You really don't care where you are going, and it doesn't matter because youjust rest and do it all over again the next day.

KostiantynVoitenko/EnvatoElements

You're sharing the jumpseat with a flight attendant that has a skincare side hustle. Every time you're strapped-in, she starts to ask you questions about your skincare routine, your hydration habits, and even starts making suggestions based on her observations. After the first duty day, she asks for your number under the guise of holding each other accountable for the early van times. Your intuition says not to give it to her, but you also don't want to seem uncooperative. As soon as the trip is over, you start receiving texts from her with skincare promotions.

As crew, we often run into situations where we make decisions against our intuition because we want to appear cooperative. This is true especially when we're with the same crew for multiple days. Being literally shoulder to shoulder with someone whom you have awkward energy with can make a 3-day trip seem like a 3-year trip. While sometimes we experience small annoyances, other times can lead to larger problems like safety risks, sexual harassment, and more.

This chapter is about boundaries. We will explore the types of boundaries and begin to define boundaries with our colleagues, passengers, family, technology, and career.

The Flow of Boundaries

Let's start out by saying that this will be a very boiler plate discussion on boundaries focused on challenges flight attendants face both professionally and personally. There are several workbooks available if you want to investigate your boundaries in a more comprehensive manner.

In general, boundaries are limits we set to define our relationships. They can be instructions on how we want to be treated. Knowing and maintaining our boundaries can improve our satisfaction in those relationships, and in the case of career boundaries, prevent burnout.

Boundaries can be described as either rigid, flexible, or porous. Imagine the air flow nobs in the passenger service unit. A completely closed vent does not allow air through; it's literally a rigid boundary. A wide-open vent allows all the air through like a porous boundary. A flexible boundary is like your hand that continually adjusts the vent to your comfort.

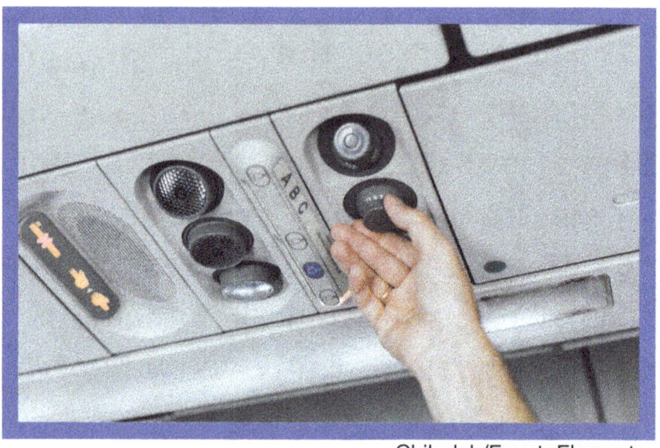

Chibelek/EnvatoElements

The type of boundaries we have will vary situationally and relationally. For example, you may be more open to talk about a health concern with your partner or best friend but not with a colleague. Conversely, you may have no issue sharing the exploits of your Vegas layover with your colleagues but not the passengers.

To help you understand your own boundaries, several exercises have been designed to assist you in contemplating how you present in various areas of your life.

Exercise 9-A
Boundaries with Colleagues

Rate the following statements to determine your boundaries with other flight attendants (non-friends) and pilots using a 1 to 5 scale: (1 - never, 2 - rarely, 3 - sometimes, 4 - very often, 5 - always).

1. If a colleague insists, I will perform tasks outside of my position's duties. ______

2. I will join the crew on a layover excursions. ______

3. I answer questions about my personal life. ______

4. I talk about my relationships on the jumpseat. ______

5. If a colleague asks for my number or personal social media, I will give it to them. ______

6. If a co-worker buys me a drink, I will drink it. ______

7. I like to give colleagues advice. ______

8. I like to joke or play pranks on colleagues. ______

9. I discuss my health conerns with colleagues. ______

10. I talk about other colleagues with my crew. ______

TOTAL ______

Total available points 50.
A low score may indicate rigid boundaries.
A high score may indicate porous boundaries.

Exercise 9-B
Boundaries with Passengers

Rate the following statements to determine your boundaries with passengers using a 1 to 5 scale:
(1 - never, 2 - rarely, 3 - sometimes, 4 - very often, 5 - always).

1. I will bend the rules rather than disappoint passengers. ______

2. I look up passengers on social media. ______

3. I answer questions about my personal life. ______

4. I talk about my relationships with passengers. ______

5. If a passenger asks for my number or personal social media, I will give it to them. ______

6. If a passenger complains enough, I give in. ______

7. I like to give passengers advice. ______

8. I like to joke or play pranks on passengers. ______

9. I discuss politics with passengers. ______

10. I talk about my crew with passengers. ______

TOTAL ______

Total available points 50.
A low score may indicate rigid boundaries.
A high score may indicate porous boundaries.

Exercise 9-C
Boundaries with Family or Partner

Rate the following statements to determine your boundaries with your family or partner using a 1 to 5 scale:
(1 - never, 2 - rarely, 3 - sometimes, 4 - very often, 5 - always).

1. If my family/partner calls, I will answer even if if passengers are on board. ______

2. I consider my family/partner first when bidding. ______

3. I check-in with my family/partner after every flight. ______

4. I share my location while I'm on the road. ______

5. I tell my family/partner about everyone that I am flying with. ______

6. I let my family/partner use my flight benefits. ______

7. I follow a strict post-trip routine. ______

8. If my family/partner wants me to stay home, I will. ______

9. I always need to know what my family/partner does. ______

10. My partner and I do not keep secrets. ______

TOTAL ______

Total available points 50.
A low score may indicate rigid boundaries.
A high score may indicate porous boundaries.

Exercise 9-D
Boundaries with Technology

Rate the following statements to determine your boundaries with technology using a 1 to 5 scale:
(1 - never, 2 - rarely, 3 - sometimes, 4 - very often, 5 - always).

1. I check my social media feeds whenever I have downtime. _____

2. I can easily spend an hour scrolling. _____

3. I must have all my notifications turned on. _____

4. I find myself getting caught up reading comments. _____

5. I find it difficult to stow my personal device while on duty. _____

6. I look at my phone as soon as I wake up. _____

7. My phone is the last thing I look at before I sleep. _____

8. I must/respond to any comment that bothers me. _____

9. I scroll my phone while out with friends. _____

10. I browse online while eating. _____

TOTAL _____

Total available points 50.
A low score may indicate rigid boundaries.
A high score may indicate porous boundaries.

Exercise 9-E
Boundaries with Your Career

Rate the following statements to determine your boundaries with your career using a 1 to 5 scale:
(1 - never, 2 - rarely, 3 - sometimes, 4 - very often, 5 - always).

1. I check open time or trade boards several times
   a day, even on days off. ______

2. I offer to assist passengers while non-reving. ______

3. I engage in social media posts about my airline. ______

4. I only take the legally required time off. ______

5. I will skip family functions if there is a good trip to
   pick up. ______

6. I engage on internal social media on days off. ______

7. I find myself talking about work on off days. ______

8. I wear airline branded clothing on off days/layovers. ______

9. I attend optional work events. ______

10. I have difficulty in non-travel related conversations. ______

TOTAL ______

Total available points 50.
A low score may indicate rigid boundaries.
A high score may indicate porous boundaries.

Exercise 9-F
Boundaries Overview

Now let's look at the big picture. You will take the total score for each domain and decide if there is anything you would like to change.

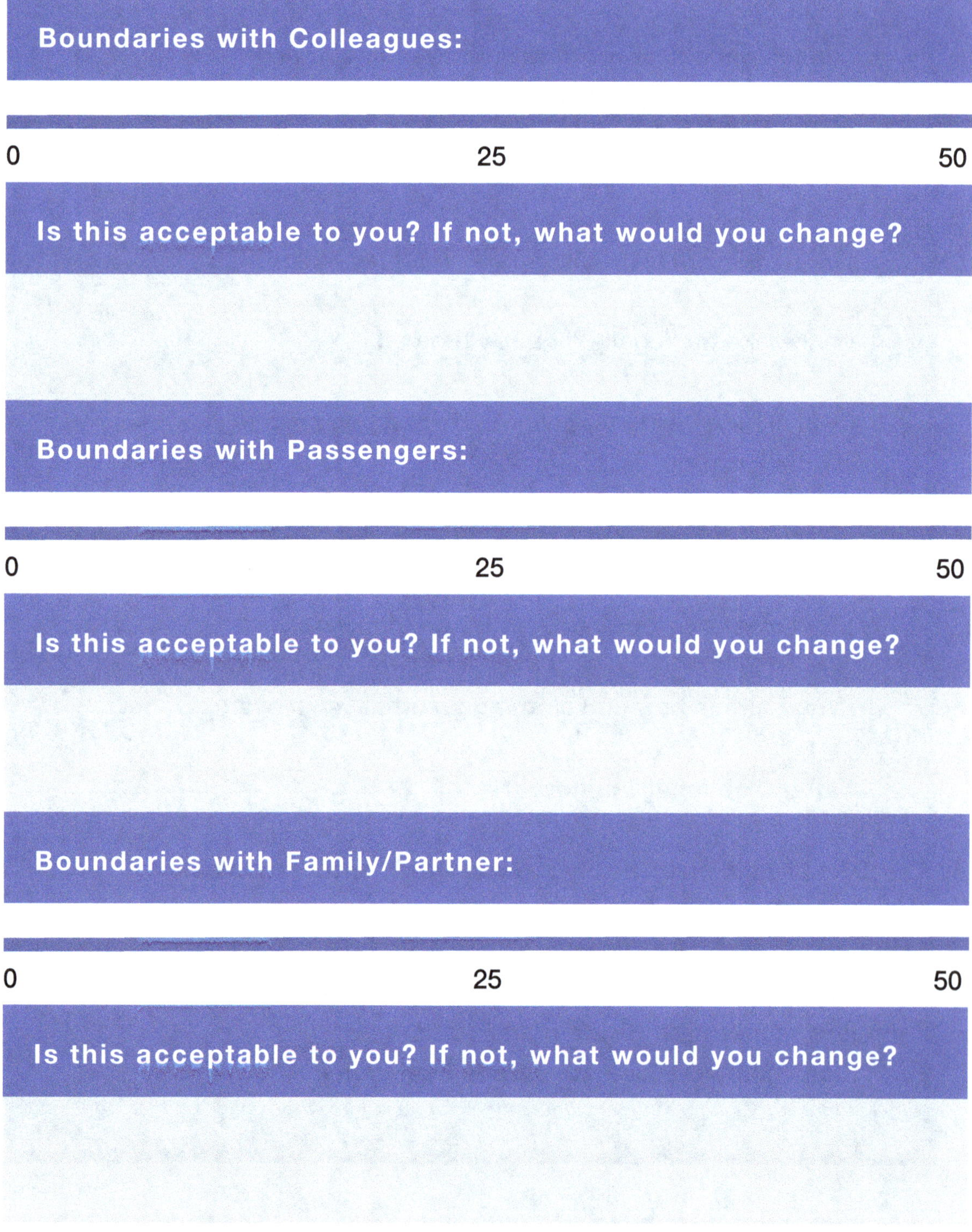

Boundaries with Technology:

0   25   50

Is this acceptable to you? If not, what would you change?

Boundaries with Your Career:

0   25   50

Is this acceptable to you? If not, what would you change?

Total Boundary Score:

0   125   250

Is this acceptable to you? If not, what would you change?

Saying "No"

In an occupation where you are expected to problem-solve to improve the passenger experience, we can often get into the trap of being a chronic people pleaser. Even when requests are against our better judgment or even company policy, we may give in just to avoid conflict or being perceived negatively.

Chronic people pleasing can make us feel exhausted, used, and have a lost sense of self. Moreover, we could put ourselves into a position of violating an FAR or being injured on the job. Here are a list of ways to say no.

Just Say "No"

- No, Thanks.
- It's against policy.
- I have a policy.
- Not today.
- That sounds nice, but I can't.
- That's not really my thing.
- Thank you for thinking of me but...
- I already have plans.
- I'm not the best person for this.
- I am already booked.
- I don't have the bandwidth at the moment.
- Not this time, sorry.
- I have to follow the rules.
- I need to take care of myself.
- I would prefer not to talk about that.
- I'm a private person.
- I have personal business to attend to.
- I'm going to pass.
- It's a no from me, dawg.

10 - The Layover

"You go to Paris every week? That sounds like heaven!" To those outside of our profession, it may seem like our career is just one big vacation. On the surface, twenty-four hours in a European city seems like plenty of time for exploration. The reality, however, is much different.

After working all night, you may need an extended nap to make up for the lost sleep. If you're a commuter, you may need a little more. By now, it's mid-afternoon. You must be careful not to stay out too late as you have a 7am wakeup call tomorrow. The return flights from Europe are always harder as the passengers are more likely to be acclimated to the time zone than the crew. After all is said and done, you may have been able to briefly sightsee, do a little shopping, and have dinner.

This chapter is all about self-care. We will explore how to build routines for restful yet fulfilling layovers, build sleep rituals at home, combat loneliness on the road, and build self-compassion. There will be tips for both the social butterfly and the slam-clicker. Whether you are staying over in Fargo or Frankfurt, you deserve to have a great time.

We're on a Budget

If there's one currency flight attendants are familiar with, it is time. Punctuality is one of the top skills needed to be successful in the career. Airplanes do not make money on the ground. Even a five-minute delay can have cascading effects throughout the operation

MargJohnsonVA/EnvatoElements

effecting rest, duty day limits, passenger connections, and aircraft routing.

In order to pull off the synchronized ballet of airline operations, employees become very familiar with understanding how long certain tasks take. For example, calculating crew breaks while anticipating service expectations. We also become hyperaware of specific dates around bidding, trades, and jumpseats.

Given the focus on time while on duty, it can become easy to just "wing-it" while on layover or off-duty. If this works for you, that's great. But, if you find yourself feeling stressed and running behind, perhaps it is time to do some time budgeting.

The first step in time budgeting is to figure out how much total time you have available to you. Then, determine the length of time required for required tasks. Don't forget any travel or preparation time for these tasks. Next, place these required tasks on your schedule. Finally, if there are any spaces, you can fill those in with optional events.

On the next page, we provide an example of a time budget for a Paris layover. You will also find a blank form you can use to try this on your own.

Exercise 10-A
Layover Plan

City	CDG
Arrival	07:15
Hotel	10:30
Van	07:15
Remain	20 hrs 45 mins

Required Tasks

Shower/Relax	1 hour
Nap	4 hours
Musée D'Orsay	2.5 hours
Dinner	2 hours
Butter Shopping	30 min
Relax/Sleep	8 hours
Morning Ritual	1.5 hours

Remain	1 hour 15 mins

Optional Activities

Boulangerie	30 min
C&A	45 min
Kusmi Tea	30 min
Eiffel Snap	30 min

Task 1		Time
	Shower/Relax	10:30

Task 2		Time
	Nap	11:30

Task 3		Time
	Boulangerie	15:30

Task 4		Time
	Musée D'Orsay	16:00

Task 5		Time
	Dinner @La Fronde	18:30

Task 6		Time
	Butter	20:30

Task 7		Time
	Relax Sleep	21:00

Task 8		Time
	Morning Ritual	05:45

Exercise 10-A
Layover Plan

City

Arrival

Hotel

Van

Remain

Required Tasks

Remain

Optional Activities

Task 1   Time

Task 2   Time

Task 3   Time

Task 4   Time

Task 5   Time

Task 6   Time

Task 7   Time

Task 8   Time

Get Some Sleep

Practicing and maintaining proper sleep hygiene is important for everyone's physical and emotional wellbeing. It is especially important for flight attendants. However, due to the lifestyle's variable schedules, it can be a challenge to maintain good sleep habits.

Traveling between time zones can disrupt circadian rhythms. Just like how we must budget time, we must also budget sleep. Sleep experts discuss the concept of a sleep bank. Unfortunately for many of us, we use it more like a sleep credit card; building debt with the hope of repaying on a long layover or an off day that allows us to sleep-in.

If we do not get enough rest, we leave ourselves susceptible to a wide range of mental and physical health problems. In addition, proper rest is important for safety professionals to be able to react in emergencies, remain alert to threats, and to protect ourselves from workplace injuries.

Garakta-Studio/EnvatoElements

One way to maintain proper rest while on the road is to build a sleep ritual. If we get into the habit of following a sleep ritual, our brain will begin to recognize the behavioral pattern and initiate the hormonal changes needed to rest. Just like how our response to a call bell is automatic, we can condition a Pavlovian response to sleep.

In the following pages, we will review tips for better sleep as well as provide examples on how to build a proper sleep routine while on layovers.

Fast Tips to Help You Sleep

- It takes one day to adjust for each hour of time zone change.
- In general, your circadian rhythm is acclimated to whatever time zone you have recently spend the most time in.
- FAR 117 provides rest and duty guidelines for pilots but the information can be useful for understanding flight attendant rest needs.
- The FAR states that if a pilot spends 72 hours in a time zone or given 36 hours of rest, they are considered acclimated.
- Caffeine has a half-life of 6 hours. This means it takes 6 hours for caffeine to lose half of its strength.
- Too much alcohol before sleep can disrupt sleep causing wakefulness in the middle of the night as it is eliminated.
- On international overnights, our sleep schedule may intersect with meal times in our acclimated time zone. Keeping a light snack handy in case of middle of the night hunger is a good idea.
- Avoid rigorous exercise 4 hours before sleep.
- Nicotine is a stimulant, avoid 4-6 hours before bed.
- Using screens before bed can interrupt circadian rhythms by fooling the brain into perceiving daylight thus delaying the release of melatonin, a sleep hormone.
- Some sleep aids can affect sleep architecture changing the amount of time we spend in various sleep stages.
- Avoid emotional and stimulating topics before bed such as watching the news or engaging in social media.
- If able, only use your bed for sleeping. If your hotel room has two beds, designate one for only sleep.
- Darkness is key for promoting quality sleep. Use blackout curtains.
- If you find yourself unable to sleep because worries or ideas pop into your head, write them down on a notepad.
- If other thoughts or a recap of your day prevents you from falling asleep, practice the Bags on a Carousel exercise in Chapter 4.

Exercise 10-B
Layover Sleep Ritual

Step One:

90 Minutes Before Bed:
Set alarm clock. Place phone on do not disturb/silent. Connect phone to charger. Lower lights in hotel room. Close curtains.

Step Two:

Wash off makeup, Brush Teeth, Take nightly supplements/medications.

Step Three:

60 Minutes Before Bed:
Warm shower or bath. Slow breathing and meditation.

Step Four:

20 Minutes Before Bed:
Enjoy a cup of chamomile tea while reading a relaxing book. Avoid using an e-book.

Exercise 10-B
Layover Sleep Ritual

Step One:

Step Two:

Step Three:

Step Four:

Tips to Fight Loneliness On Trips

Keep photos of loved ones such as family or pets handy and accessible. Visual reminders can ground us, and remind us who is looking forward to our return.

meteoritka/EnvatoElements

Watch a familiar show. Studies have shown that when we rewatch a favorite show, the familiarity with the characters can combat loneliness. (Derrick, J.E., et al., 2009).

Media_photos/EnvatoElements

Phone a friend. Reconnect with familiar faces by calling a trusted friend. If you call your partner, do not talk about things that have to be done upon your return.

jacoblund/EnvatoElements

Exercise 10-C
Building Self-Compassion

We can easily become our biggest bully if we engage in negative self-talk. Surprisingly, we wouldn't accept these harsh judgments from others but we do from ourselves. Use the form below to record negative self-talk and replace with positive beliefs.

Negative Self-Talk Statement	Rate Believability (0-10)	Would You Accept This From a Friend? (Y/N)	Replace with a Positive Observation
I mess everything up. I can't do anything right.	8	N	I've had successes. I'm working my dream job.

Additional Comments:

Exercise 10-D
Post-Trip Inventory

Use this form to debrief from a trip. Your results can help inform your future schedule bids.

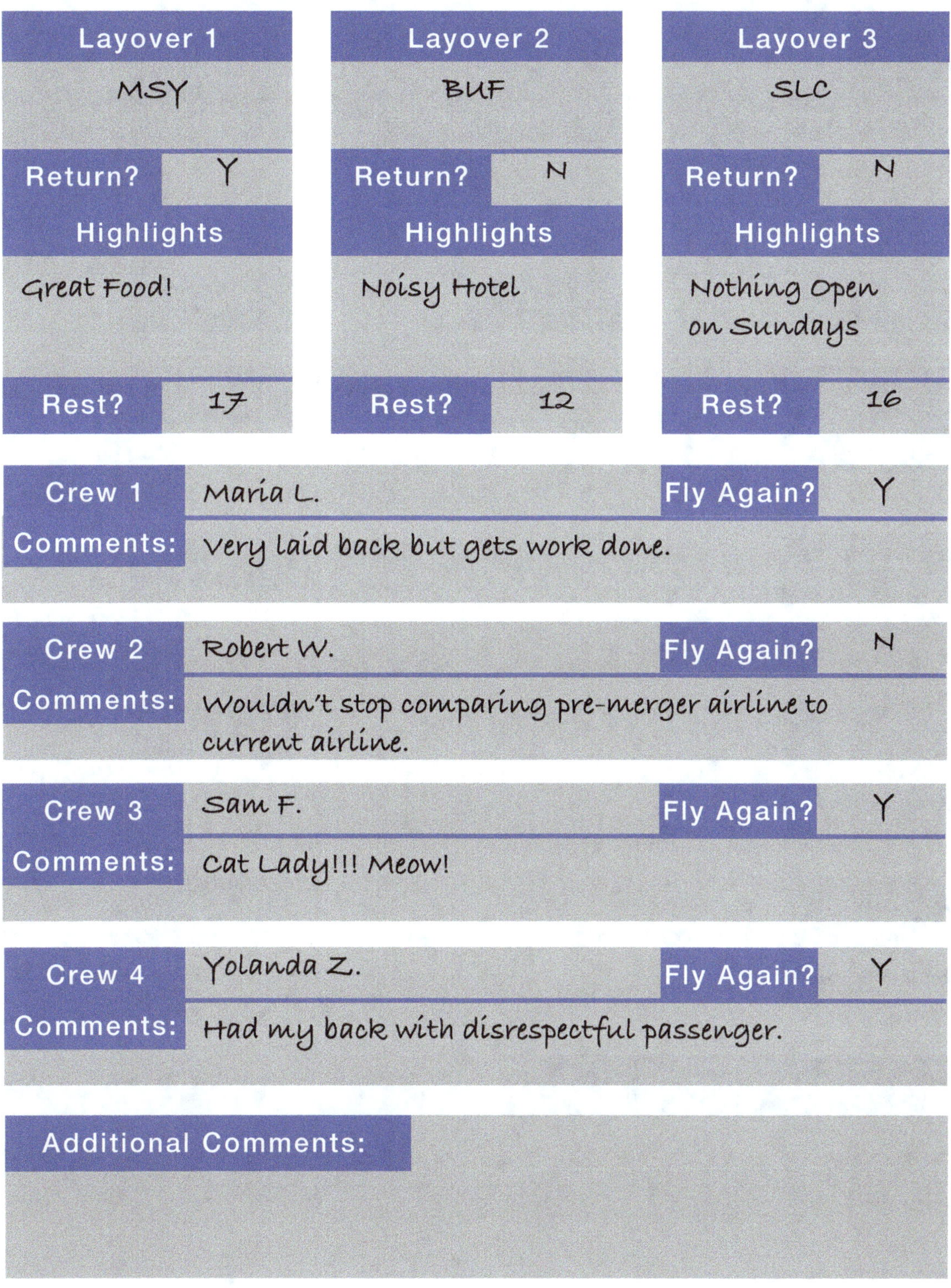

Exercise 10-D
Post-Trip Inventory

Layover 1

Return?

Highlights

Rest?

Layover 2

Return?

Highlights

Rest?

Layover 3

Return?

Highlights

Rest?

Crew 1

Fly Again?

Comments:

Crew 2

Fly Again?

Comments:

Crew 3

Fly Again?

Comments:

Crew 4

Fly Again?

Comments:

Additional Comments:

11 - Crew Dynamics

You just boarded an aircraft after attending a crew briefing for an international departure. The purser reviewed the details of the flight and reviewed service standards and expectations. The purser highlighted that even though the flight is full, the eye masks and menus should be hand-delivered to passengers in economy as per the airline's service standard.

After stowing your luggage and performing your safety checks, you begin to prepare the cabin for boarding. A senior flight attendant hands you a stack of menus and tells you to put one on each seat. You state that you thought they were to be hand-delivered.

The other flight attendant acknowledges the request but states, "The flight is full. I'm not climbing over people to hand out menus."

On one hand, you want to follow the standards. On the other hand, you will be directly working with this other flight attendant for the entire trip. Additionally, you know the purser will be too busy with boarding in business class to pay attention to economy.

Scenarios like this play out daily at every airline. Although it's imperative for flight attendants to work together, due to the shuffling of crews, many crewmembers are just meeting each other for the first time at briefing. This creates a phenomenon in which a social heirarchy forms.

In this chapter, we will explore crew dynamics through the theory of group formation. With this knowledge, we may be better able to understand why some of our colleagues do what they do.

Stages of Group Formation

Just like a flight has various stages such as boarding, take-off, cruise, descent, and landing, groups also have various stages. Psychologist Bruce Tuckman (1965) conceptualized group development into four phases: forming, storming, norming, and performing. Let's explore each of these stages as it applies to crew dynamics.

Forming

In group development, forming is when group members first come together to learn about challenges and opportunities that lie ahead. The team then beings to develop a common goal and responsibilities are delegated to help achieve this. More experienced members may begin to model appropriate behavior for the less experienced members.

In crew dynamics, this stage is when the crew first meets. Whether you are flying a domestic trip where the crew briefly meets on the aircraft, or an international itinerary with a more intense pre-departure briefing, this stage can set the tone for the rest of the trip. First impressions mean a lot in this stage. One of the biggest challenges in this phase is for crew in non-leadership roles to relinquish control and for flight leaders to realize that not all crewmembers may be familiar with the nuances of their style.

Reflect on a crew briefing that made you wish you just stayed at home. What made it so difficult?

Storming

Storming is the phase when challenges arise. Members may test the limits of authority by doing tasks how they want instead of how the leader designated. Group hierarchy is formed, and roles begin to be defined. Disagreements, power struggles, and alliances may form. This phase does not happen with all groups, but when it does, it requires strong leadership to move through it.

When working as a flight attendant, this phase usually occurs once on-board, but may start as soon as the briefing. After crewmembers settle in, they may default to their way of doing things. In the example at the beginning of this chapter, a flight attendant may just ignore instructions. Depending on the level of attunement the flight leaders have to their crew, this phase may end before take-off or last through the entire first service.

Reflect on a time when your crew was not working in harmony. What happened? What could have prevented this?

Norming

Norming is the stage of group development where standards are normalized throughout the group. In the case where there is weak leadership, this phase may feel like a protracted version of storming, where chaos and anarchy are the norm for the group. Other times, this is when a leader has addressed concerns, mediated conflict, and enforced behavioral limits.

As crew, this is the phase when the crew moves from defining their roles to operating within them. If a flight leader has detected and mitigated inconsistencies, this is when the crew begins to operate according to standard. Crewmembers feel comfortable speaking up when they see inconsistencies from colleagues.

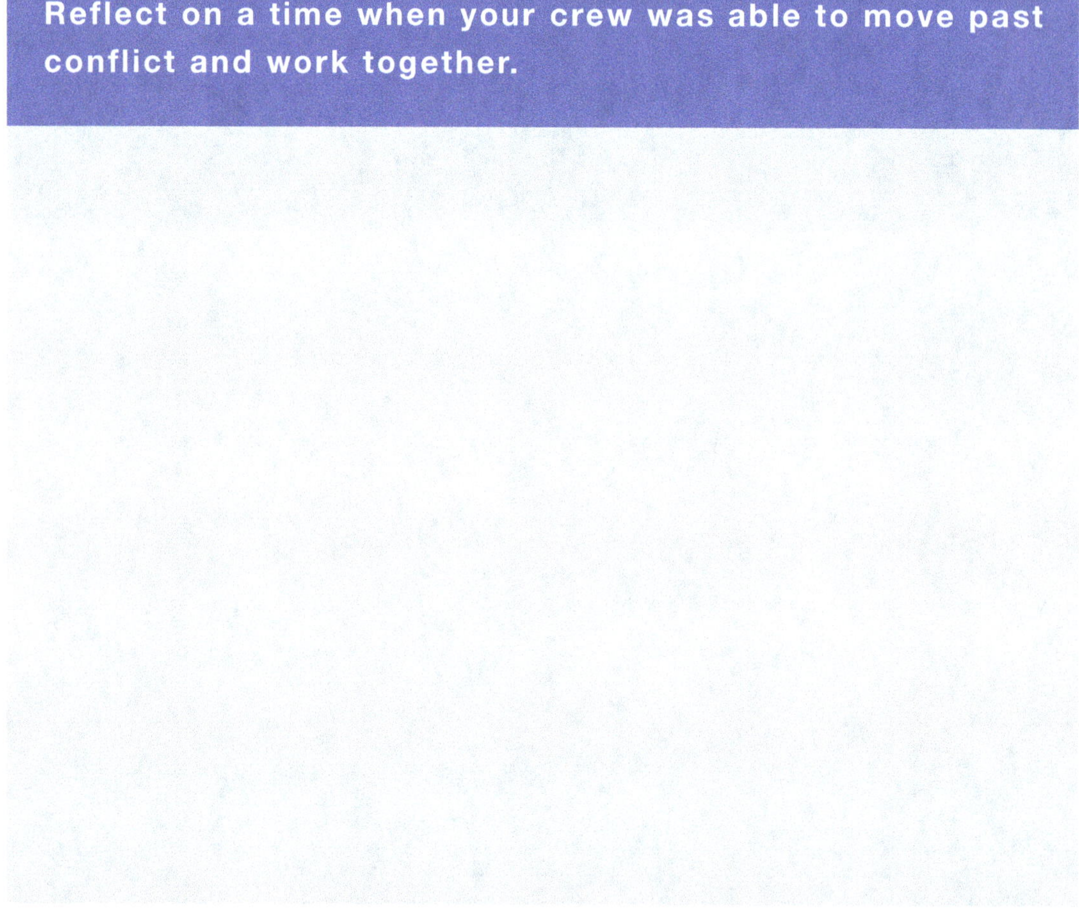

Performing

When a group enters the performing stage, group norms have been established and roles defined. The group is focused on a common goal and is working towards it. Less redirection is needed from leadership.

If a crew has successfully progressed through the previous three stages, a crew will reach the performing stage. Think of it like being on autopilot. The crew knows what is expected of them and performs the tasks without much guidance. This is where you know your colleagues' areas of strength and weakness. For example, some flight attendants are better at diplomatically addressing problematic passenger behavior. If trouble erupts in the cabin, the crew will know which member to call on to address the conflict.

Regression

A group may regress to a previous phase when there have been changes. Irregular operations and crew scheduling changes may facilitate a change in crew complement.

Recall a time you witnessed a phase regression from your crew. What do you believe caused it?

Additional Factors

It is important to address additional factors that can affect crew dynamics. Flight attendants are usually one of the largest, if not the largest, workgroup at an airline. Therefore, each crew complement comes with a wide range of backgrounds and experience. For some, this may be their first and only airline that they have worked for. For others, this is a career change. And of course, there are the flight attendants who have worked for many airlines and have experienced mergers, bankruptcies, and the rollercoaster-like ups and downs this industry has to offer.

Remember that each flight attendant's unique experience brings a fresh perspective to the job. A colleague discussing how things used to be done may not actually be pining for their old airline but rather they are coping with the many changes they have experienced in their long-storied career. A junior flight attendant that gets excited over standard operations should be allowed their enthusiasm. We were all junior stews at some point in time. Would our younger selves have liked someone raining on our parade?

svitlanah/envatoelements

Exercise 11-A
Best and Worst Awards

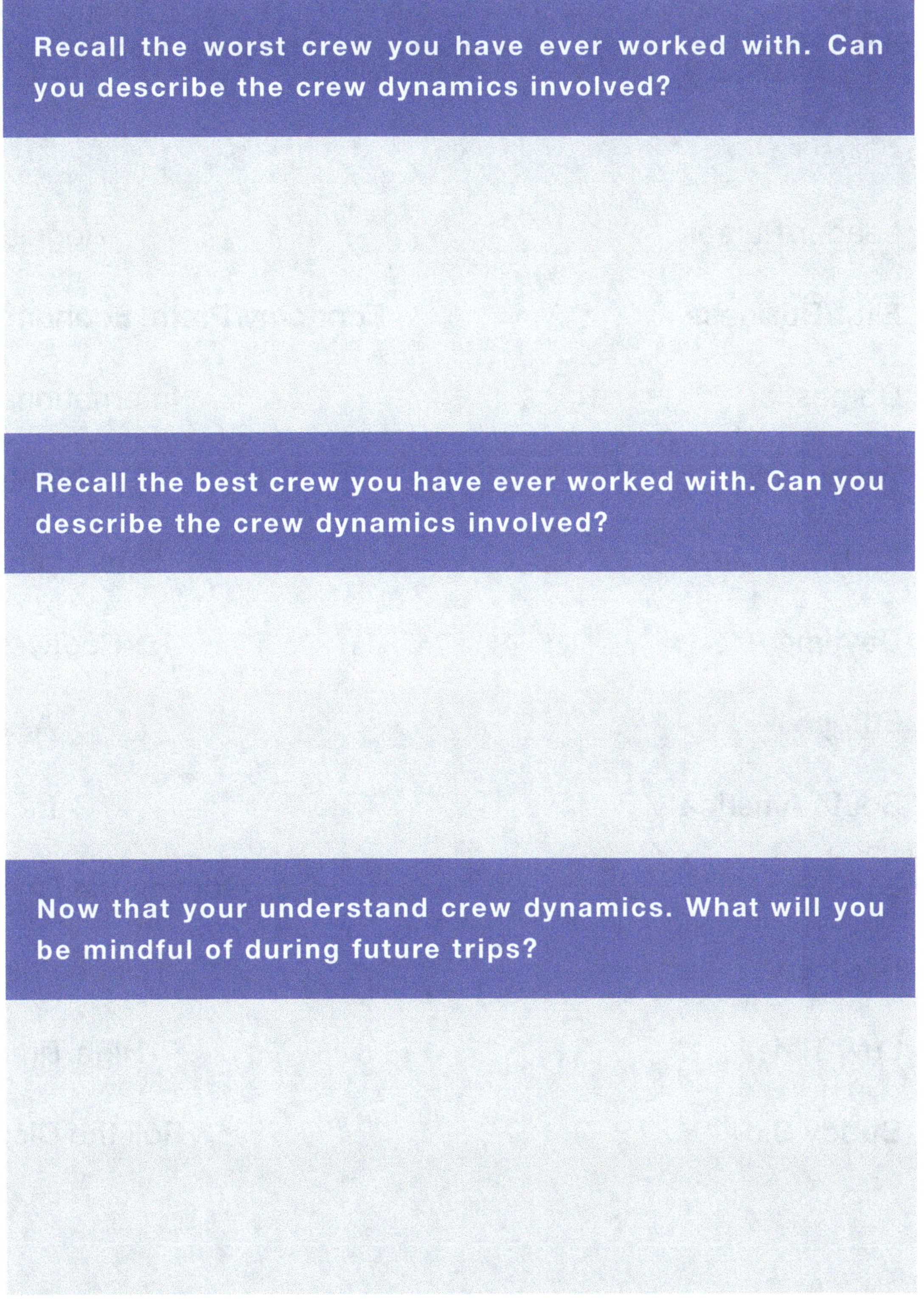

Exercise 11-B
My Working Style

Circle your working preferences. Compare to a work friend. You don't have to have the same preferences to make a compatible crew.

Leader/Purser	Regular
First/Business	Economy/Prem. Economy
Domestic	International
Turns	Overnights
Early Mornings	Late Nights
Daytime	Redeyes
Europe	Asia
South America	Africa
Lone Wolf	Go with the Flow
Reserve	Lineholder
Low Time	High Time
Buddy Bid	Roll the Dice

Bonus Activities

Fun flying related activities to de-stress and reflect.

kit8/envatoelements

Aircraft Checklist

Circle or highlight the aircraft you have worked.

A220	B757	EMB123
A300	B767	ERJ135
A310	B777	ERJ145
A318	B787	E175
A319	BA146	E190
A320	Caravelle	F28
A321	Concorde	F100
A330	Constellation	JS41
A340	CRJ200	L1011
A350	CRJ550	MD11
A380	CRJ700	MD80/8
ATR 42/72	CRJ900	MD90
B707	CRJ1000	Q400
B717	DC8	SAAB340
B727	DC9	SAAB2000
B737	DC10	SSJ100
B747	DH-8	328JET

Commuting Bingo

Relatively Empty Flight	First Flight Option is Full	Last Minute Passengers	Randomly Selected for Security	Flying on a Competitor
Regretting Wearing Your Uniform	Passenger Concerned About Their Connection	You Know the Crew	Passenger Lined Up Before In-bound Has Arrived	Crew Brings You Water
KCM Closed	Someone Hands You Trash	FREE SPACE	Middle Seat	Delayed Flight
International Flight	Crew Brings You Food	Gossiping in the Galley	Gate Agent Soliciting to Check Bags	Chatty Seatmate
On Time Flight	Pilots Say Hello	Arrival Gate is Occupied	Upgrade	Crying Baby

Crew Bingo

"When I worked at ________ Airlines"	The Side Hustle FA	Flying with Friends	You're the Most Junior	The Flirty FA
Dad Jokes from Pilots	Camping in the Last Row	You're the Most Senior	"I don't fly ________."	The Galley Guard
"I set up my carts this way."	Pilots Introduce Themselves	FREE SPACE	Brings All Their Own Food	Jumpseat Therapy
Gossiping in the Galley	The Influencer FA	FA Calling Romantic Partner	The Cat FA	The Commuter with 1000 Bags.
"These newhires are ________."	The Prankster	Former CEO was Better.	"I'm Pre-Merger ________."	Newhire on the Crew

Celebrity List

Use this page to keep track of the celebrities you've had as guests on your flights.

deemakdaksinas/envatoelements

Keeping It Fresh

Keep your job fresh by learning to have a little fun a work. Try out any of the above suggestions. A little silliness won't hurt.

Try a New Hairstyle

Wear Your Watch on the Opposite Arm

Work a Different Position

Try a New Restaurant

Wear a New Uniform Piece

Skip the Train and Walk to the Gate

Eat Your Dessert First

Ask a Passenger to Suggest a Drink

Fly a Different Route

Ask a Passenger for Layover Recommendations

____

____

____

____

The Airplane

Imagine an airplane full of passengers. Some of the passengers are "problem" passengers who sneak their own alcohol on, get up in the middle of service, and listen to shows without headphones. There are also  "good" passengers on board who follow directions, are considerate of others, and keep their shoes on. The rest are just "average" passengers who sit in their seats and go unnoticed.

At the front of the plane is the lead flight attendant who has to keep redirecting the "problem" passenger behavior and maybe giving an extra snack or two to the good passengers.

Your thoughts and feelings are like the passengers in the cabin: some a negative, some positive, and some neutral. Some will do everything in their power to get your attention even if you don't want to interact with them at the moment. There's also a part of you that tries to manage all of this like the lead flight attendant.

Who are you in this metaphor?

Most people will pick the lead flight attendant. But take a moment and visualize yourself as the entire airplane. You hold all these passengers and crew, but you are also separate from them. You don't have to get bogged down trying to manage each passenger's behavior. Just like you don't have to get caught up in managing each thought.

Description vs Evaluation

This exercise is designed to help you differentiate between descriptive self-talk and evaluative self talk.

Look at the piece of luggage below:

What if I told you that this is the best piece of luggage in the world? Would you believe me? How could you be sure?

As you can see, evaluative statements and statements of worth such as "best" "worst" "worthless" "terrible" "ugly" are all subjective while facts are objective and can be verified.

Evaluative self-statements such as:
"I am worthless." "I am lazy." "I'm a terrible person." are nothing more than unverifiable opinions.

Write an evaluative self-statement here:

Evidence For: **Evidence Against:**

Stop Resisting

This is a radical acceptance exercise designed to demonstrate the difference between resisting uncomfortable sensations, thoughts, and feelings versus accepting them.

Take a moment and get strapped into the jumpseat. Make sure you tighten the harness as tight as you can, just like they showed you in initial training. So tight that you feel like you've become one with the seat.

Now for the next two minutes, do everything possible to avoid feeling the tightness of the harness. Whenever you notice a feeling of constriction or stiffness, resist the feeling.

How much effort did you have to put in to resisting a sensation that is literally touching you?

Let's try this same exercise again. But this time, you will welcome the feelings of tightness and constriction. Whenever you notice a feeling of being unable to move, welcome it.

How was this part of the exercise different for you?

Airline Industry Word Search

```
H M Y R D E L A Y L E P U R S E R Y
X I K E O Y H B A L T I T U D E P S
C N C R J L I N E H O L D E R A I C
O D M O I B D R E S E R V E W V L H
M F K U S E C U R I T Y U U A Z O E
M U S T A I R L I N E K C R E W T D
U L K E C I M C G A T E A G E N T U
T N F L I G H T A T T E N D A N T L
E E U B X S A F E T Y R D C W Q Y I
E S U N X V C R A S H P A D X L L N
M S M O J U M P S E A T P F W M B G
X M J A F I R S T A I D U H N T H T
```

WORD LIST

AIRLINE	GATE AGENT	SAFETY
ALTITUDE	JUMPSEAT	SCHEDULING
COMMUTE	LINEHOLDER	SECURITY
CRASHPAD	MINDFULNESS	
CREW	PILOT	
DELAY	PURSER	
FIRST AID	REROUTE	
FLIGHT ATTENDANT	RESERVE	

Next Stop

References

AFA-CWA. (2024). #MeToo in the Air. Association of Flight Attendants. https://www.afacwa.org/metoo

Centers for Disease Control and Prevention. (2023, February 24). Aircrew Safety and Health. Centers for Disease Control and Prevention https://www.cdc.gov/niosh/topics/aircrew/default.html

Climate Central. (2023, December 5). Climate change is disrupting air travel. Climate Change is Disrupting Air Travel | Climate Central. https://www.climatecentral.org/climate-matters/climate-change-is-disrupting-air-travel-2023

Derrick, Jaye & Gabriel, Shira & Hugenberg, Kurt. (2009). Social surrogacy: How favored television programs provide the experience of be longing. Journal of Experimental Social Psychology. 45. 352-362. 10.1016/j.jesp.2008.12.003.

Federal Aviation Administration. (2023, August 8). FAA Refers More Unruly Passenger Cases to FBI. FAA Newsroom. Retrieved February 19, 2024, from https://www.faa.gov/newsroom/faa-refers-more-unruly-passenger-cases-fbi.

Harris, R. (2019). Act made simple: An easy-to-read primer on acceptance and commitment therapy (2nd ed.). New Harbinger Publications, Inc.

Linehan, M. (2015). DBT skills training handouts and worksheets. The Guilford Press.

Maiello, M. L. (2010). NCRP report no. 160: Ionizing radiation exposure of the population of the United States. Health Physics, 98(3), 549–550. https://doi.org/10.1097/hp.0b013e3181c80d20

McNeely, E., Mordukhovich, I., Tideman, S., Gale, S., & Coull, B. (2018). Estimating the health consequences of flight attendant work: Compar ing flight attendant health to the general population in a cross-sectional study. BMC Public Health, 18(1). https://doi.org/10.1186/s12889-018-5221-3

Newell, J. M. & MacNeil, G. A. (2010). Professional burnout, vicarious trauma, secondary traumatic stress, and compassion fatigue: A review of theoretical terms, risk factors, and preventive methods for clinicians andsearchers. Best Practices in Mental Health, 6(2), 57-68

Tuckman, B. W. (1965). Developmental sequence in small groups. Psycho logical Bulletin, 63(6), 384–399. https://doi.org/10.1037/h0022100